SIX CHARACTERS
IN SEARCH OF AN AUTHOR

THE DRAMA LIBRARY

General Editor: EDWARD THOMPSON

SIX CHARACTERS IN SEARCH OF AN AUTHOR

by

LUIGI PIRANDELLO

Translated by
FREDERICK MAY

HEINEMANN EDUCATIONAL BOOKS
LONDON

Heinemann Educational Books Ltd.
LONDON EDINBURGH MELBOURNE AUCKLAND TORONTO
HONG KONG SINGAPORE KUALA LUMPUR NEW DELHI
NAIROBI JOHANNESBURG LUSAKA IBADAN
KINGSTON

ISBN 0 435 20720 2

First published in this translation 1954
Reprinted 1958, 1960, 1964, 1966, 1968, 1969, 1971,
1973, 1975, 1976

Published by
Heinemann Educational Books Ltd
48 Charles Street, London W1X 8AH
Printed Offset Litho and bound in Great Britain by
Cox & Wyman Ltd, London, Fakenham and Reading

INTRODUCTION

by

FREDERICK MAY

LUIGI PIRANDELLO was born at Caos, near Girgenti (the modern Agrigento) in Sicily, on June 28th, 1867. At the age of nineteen after having worked for three months in the family sulphur business, he persuaded his father to allow him to study letters at the University of Palermo, from where he proceeded, in 1887, to the University of Rome. Here he had the good fortune to work under, and to gain the friendship of the eminent scholar, Monaci, and when an irreparable quarrel broke out between Pirandello and the Professor of Latin, it was Monaci who counselled the young man to proceed to Bonn and there to complete his studies under the distinguished philologist, Wendelin Foerster.

He gained his doctorate with a thesis on the dialect of Girgenti in 1891, and after a further period at Bonn as lector in Italian he returned to Rome, where he quite soon became a prominent member of the group of writers and artists who revolved around Luigi Capuana, the novelist and critic, for already Pirandello was beginning to be considered one of the more serious of the anti-D'Annunzian young authors.

A disciple of the great verist short-story writer, playwright and novelist, Giovanni Verga, whose compassionate preoccupation with the anguish and the agony of man he shares, he impatiently and vehemently rejected D'Annunzio's cult of the superman; and the austere purity and unrhetorical dignity of his style are in vigorous contrast with the morbid sensuality, the exoticism and the high-flown rhetoric of the older writer. D'Annunzio, and frequently magnificently so, is the poet of sensation, while Pirandello is the poet of experience.

His first published work, *Mal Giocondo* (1889), was a collection of poems very reminiscent of Leopardi and of Carducci; it was followed by other volumes of poetry, by the publication of his thesis and by a handful of novels and a stream of short stories. Pirandello excels in the short story form and it is possible that with the sole exception of Verga he may ultimately be ranked as the finest Italian writer in that medium after Boccaccio. Of his novels, *The Late Mathias Pascal* (1904), is undoubtedly the most important. A most moving and highly original work, it is Pirandello's first major statement of the theme of being and seeming which, under a multitude of aspects, he developed with such power and urgency in his plays. From it may be said to stem the entire *grotesque*[1] movement in Italian drama, a movement which was to find its natural fulfilment in the plays of Pirandello himself, as it was to find its æsthetic in his essay, *Humour*.

In 1894 he married Antonietta Portulano in obedience to his father's wishes. Though very much a marriage determined by the commercial interests of the parents, it was nonetheless during the first few years a happy one and three children were born. Then came financial disaster which, following upon a severe illness brought on by the difficult birth of her last child, seriously affected the mind of Antonietta Pirandello. She became steadily more and more insane, constantly and unreasonably jealous, and until 1919, when she entered a nursing-home, Pirandello's life was unceasing torment.

In 1898 he published his first play, *The Vice*, but it was not until 1915, the year in which James Joyce first introduced his work to English readers, that he began to write seriously for the theatre, and only in 1921 did he achieve any real success. *Six Characters in Search of an Author*, rapidly followed by *Henry IV*, made him famous throughout the world and made it possible for him to give up his academic work. For poverty had obliged

[1] *The Mask and the Face* by Luigi Chiarelli, a savage comedy treating of the conflict between illusion and reality in love and in marriage, is perhaps the most typical GROTESQUE and certainly the one best known in England. Schnitzler's *The Green Cockatoo* is also a GROTESQUE and Barrie's *Dear Brutus* and Synge's *The Playboy of the Western World* may with some justice be said to belong to the genre.

him to lecture in a teacher-training college for women, a form of drudgery which is amply satirised in his earlier work.

Pirandello once remarked that he had no life outside his writing; and like so many of his characters he could sadly affirm that for himself he was nobody; he was whatever you wished him to be. An interesting entry occurs in his private notebook for 1933–34, "There is someone who is living my life. And I know nothing about him." A man of great gentleness and humility, his deepest concern is always with humankind and always most with those who are defeated by life—the grey, ordinary people—people like the Father, the Mother and the Stepdaughter. Like Charlie Chaplin, he cuts with irony through the illusions of th: conventional, social being to the persistent goodness of authentic man, finding, as did Leopardi, the abiding bond in a communion of pity. Leopardian, too, is his perception of the paradox that it is the bitterness of life that forces upon us a sense of wonderment at the beauty of life. As he wrote to the American critic, Vittorini, "A man, I have tried to tell something to other men, without any ambition, except perhaps that of avenging myself for having been born. And yet, life, in spite of all that it has made me suffer, is so beautiful!"

In 1925 Pirandello attempted to found a national theatre at the Teatro Odescalchi in Rome and whilst artistically he triumphed, financially his enterprise was a failure. In 1934 he was awarded the Nobel Prize for Literature and on December 10th, 1936, he died suddenly in Rome. His last wish is typical of his radiant austerity: he asked that the utmost simplicity should be observed at his funeral—*The hearse, the horse, the driver—nothing more.*

Pirandello wrote some forty-three plays in Italian[1] and with them he so enriched the material of the drama and so recast its techniques of communication, giving them a new precision and a new immediacy, that Eric Bentley has properly set him among the great innovators and masters of his craft. And T. S. Eliot has said, "Pirandello is a dramatist to whom all serious dramatists, of my generation and the next, must recognise a debt

[1] He also wrote plays in Sicilian.

of gratitude. He has taught us something about what our problems are, and indicated directions in which their solution may be sought. He has shown us by his example that the escape from the confinement of naturalistic realism in the theatre need not be sought in the artificially 'poetic' or in the fantasies of a play of bloodless ideas and arid epigrams. He has had the courage and the imagination which have made it possible to penetrate 'realism' and arrive at reality."

Pirandello shows how in terms of theatre the intellect may be converted into passion. He extends the frontiers of the drama by giving effective dramatic shape and emotionally significant utterance to metaphysical concepts, transforming ideas into cogent, living people who provoke our interest and compel our sympathy; they are in fact our secret lives made manifest. And in doing this Pirandello creates a new kind of tragedy, of which *Henry IV* and *Six Characters in Search of an Author* are major examples. It is an ironic tragedy, the tragedy of man tormented by the enigma of personality, perplexed by the impossibility of arriving at truth, and for ever questioning the nature and the purpose of existence; he knows a need to fix his being in some comfortably definite form, yet the relentless ever-flowing life-force sweeps away the tawdry frailty of his every construction; illusion after illusion vanishes under his scrutiny; and he achieves intelligence only to recognise that he can communicate with no one, not even with himself, and that no one can communicate with him—that he is, in the fullest sense, alone.

Pirandello is, in fact, interpreting in theatrical terms the world of Freud, of Jung and of Einstein. He dramatises the sub-conscious; his events are the discoveries, the realisations and the awarenesses of the mind. From them he has constructed a drama of experience, subtle and lucid, and penetratingly human. His technique is admirably apt to his undertaking and few modern dramatists are his equal in play construction or in the delineation of character. *Six Characters in Search of an Author* is an excellent example of his craftsmanship, a play well-made, not by any mechanical standards, but because in it is to be observed a smooth, organic growth, every situation arising logically, not from a preconceived plan in the author's mind, but from the whole life of the play till then, and meeting the inevitable demands which that life makes upon the future. And his dialogue, terse, direct and immediately evocative, catching the rhythms of ordinary everyday speech, yet poetic in its concentration and suggestiveness, is a perfect vehicle for his drama.

Whilst the lyric tragedies, *Henry IV* and *No One Knows Why*, are perhaps Pirandello's masterpieces, central to his work as a dramatist is his trilogy of the theatre (*Six Characters in Search of an Author*, *Each in His Own Way* and *To-night We Improvise*) in which he examines the nature, the quality and the implications of the conflicts which arise between the elements that make up the theatre. They are, writes the Belgian dramatist, Crommelynck, "the panels of a triptych. . . . These three works, consecrated to the drama of Man in search of God, of Man striving to know the Nature and the Will of God, will, if they are better understood, bring us to a full realisation of his genius." Considerable too, are the acerb comedy, *Liolà*, Machiavellian in its astringency, *Diana and Tuda*, in which he portrays the rebellion of life against the rigidity of art, *As You Desire Me*, a savage denunciation of modern civilisation as something so brutish as to be incompatible and irreconcilable with the aspirations of the human spirit, *Right You Are (If You Think So)*, a satirical amalgam of tragedy and social comedy, and the one-act plays, *The Man with the Flower in His Mouth* and *A Dream (But Perhaps Not)*.

Six Characters in Search of an Author has become a classic. It has endured, not because of any novelty of form, strikingly original though that form is, but because its vision of life is profound and entire, and because it deals with the whole man alive; its form is the inevitable consequence of its content and a miracle of crystallisation. We are enabled simultaneously to see at every moment past, present and future and plane upon plane of reality. The mood of the play is tragedy, but tragedy blended with satire of the romantic drama, high comedy and even farce. And the implicit thesis has been admirably summed up by Desmond MacCarthy, "Signor Pirandello has illustrated what every profound dramatist must feel when he sees his characters on the stage; his sufferings at the inevitable distortions due to the substitution of the personality of the actor for that of his character as he imagined it. But he has done more than that. He has suggested the inevitable limitations of the modern drama, the falsifications which result from cramming scenes into acts and tying incidents down to times and places. And he has done more yet; in an odd way he has suggested that the fate of many people is not unlike those of the 'Characters' in the play; that many of us are in their predicament, namely, like them, real enough people, for whom fate nevertheless has not written the plays in which we might have played a part.''

One thing I would add: Pirandello makes us vividly aware of how infinitely more real are the characters than the so-called real people of everyday life, the producer and his actors. They are life, the quintessential distillation of all human life at all times.

Six Characters in Search of an Author is, I suggest, the dramatic analogue of *The Waste Land*. Each is a high poetic record of the disillusionment and spiritual desolation of its time, instinct with compassion and poignant with the sense of loss; each finds its dynamic in the Christian consciousness which is emergent within it; each has become in its own sphere at once the statement and the symbol of its age, unique in tone and arresting in accent; and each has been astonishingly fertile, creating a new world of drama and a new world of poetry.

This translation has been made from the definitive text of *Sei personaggi in cerca d'autore*, which differs considerably from Pirandello's first version of the play, originally published in 1921. This is the first translation to be published, I believe, which is based on Pirandello's final text.

SIX CHARACTERS
IN SEARCH OF AN AUTHOR

A PLAY IN THE MAKING

THE CHARACTERS OF THE PLAY IN THE MAKING

THE FATHER
THE MOTHER
THE STEPDAUGHTER
THE SON
THE BOY (non-speaking)
THE LITTLE GIRL (non-speaking)
MADAME PACE (who is called into being)

THE ACTORS IN THE COMPANY

THE PRODUCER
THE LEADING LADY
THE LEADING MAN
THE SECOND FEMALE LEAD[1]
THE INGENUE
THE JUVENILE LEAD
OTHER ACTORS AND ACTRESSES
THE STAGE MANAGER
THE PROMPTER
THE PROPERTY MAN
THE FOREMAN OF THE STAGE CREW
THE PRODUCER'S SECRETARY
THE COMMISSIONAIRE
STAGE HANDS AND OTHER THEATRE PERSONNEL

([1] She is referred to as THE SECOND ACTRESS in the text.)

DAYTIME: THE STAGE OF A THEATRE

N.B.—The play has neither acts nor scenes. Its performance will be interrupted twice: once—though the curtain will not be lowered—when the PRODUCER and the principal CHARACTERS go away to write the script and the ACTORS leave the stage, and a second time when the Man on the Curtain lets it fall by mistake.

When the audience enters the auditorium the curtain is up and the stage is just as it would be during the daytime. There is no set and there are no wings; it is empty and in almost total darkness. This is in order that right from the very beginning the audience shall receive the impression of being present, not at a performance of a carefully rehearsed play, but at a performance of a play that suddenly happens.

Two small flights of steps, one right and one left, give access to the stage from the auditorium.

On the stage itself, the prompter's dome has been removed, and is standing just to one side of the prompt box.

Downstage, on the other side, a small table and an armchair with its back turned to the audience have been set for the Producer.

Two more small tables, one rather larger than the other, together with several chairs, have been set downstage so that they are ready if needed for the rehearsal. There are other chairs scattered about to the left and to the right for the actors, and, in the background, to one side and almost hidden, there is a piano.

When the house lights go down the FOREMAN *comes on to the stage through the door back. He is dressed in blue dungarees and carries his tools in a bag slung at his belt. From a corner at the back of the stage he takes one or two slats of wood, brings them down front, kneels down and starts nailing them together. At the sound of his hammer the* STAGE-MANAGER *rushes in from the direction of the dressing-rooms.*

STAGE-MANAGER: Hey! What are you doing?

FOREMAN: What am I doing? Hammering . . . nails.

STAGE-MANAGER: At this time of day? (*He looks at his watch.*) It's gone half-past ten! The Producer'll be here any minute now and he'll want to get on with his rehearsal.

FOREMAN: And let me tell *you* something . . . I've got to have time to do *my* work, too.

STAGE-MANAGER: You'll get it, you'll get it. . . . But you can't do that *now*.

FOREMAN: When can I do it then?

STAGE-MANAGER: After the rehearsal. Now, come on. . . .

Clear up all this mess, and let me get on with setting the second act of *The Game As He Played It*.

(*The* FOREMAN *gathers his pieces of wood together, muttering and grumbling all the while, and goes off. Meanwhile, the* ACTORS OF THE COMPANY *have begun to come on to the stage through the door back. First one comes in, then another, then two together . . . just as they please. There are nine or ten of them in all—as many as you would suppose you would need for the rehearsal of Pirandello's play,* The Game As He Played It, *which has been called for today. As they come in they greet one another and the* STAGE-MANAGER *with a cheery 'Good morning'. Some of them go off to their dressing-rooms; others, and among them the* PROMPTER, *who is carrying the prompt copy rolled up under his arm, remain on the stage, waiting for the* PRODUCER *to come and start the rehearsal. While they are waiting— some of them standing, some seated about in small groups—they exchange a few words among themselves. One lights a cigarette, another complains about the part that he's been given and a third reads out an item of news from a theatrical journal for the benefit of the other actors. It would be best if all the* ACTORS AND ACTRESSES *could be dressed in rather bright and gay clothes. This first improvised scene should be played very naturally and with great vivacity. After a while, one of the comedy men can sit down at the piano and start playing a dance-tune. The younger* ACTORS AND ACTRESSES *start dancing.*)

STAGE-MANAGER (*clapping his hands to restore order*): Come on, now, come on! That's enough of that! Here's the producer!

(*The music and dancing come to a sudden stop. The* ACTORS *turn and look out into the auditorium and see the* PRODUCER, *who is coming in through the door. He comes up the gangway between the stalls, bowler hat on head, stick under arm, and a large cigar in his mouth, to the accompaniment of a chorus of 'Good-mornings' from the* ACTORS *and climbs up one of the flights of steps on to the stage. His* SECRETARY *offers him his post—a newspaper or so, a script.*)

PRODUCER: Any letters?

SECRETARY: None at all. This is all the post there is.

PRODUCER (*handing him back the script*): Put it in my office.

(*Then, looking around and turning to the* STAGE-MANAGER.) Oh, you can't see a thing here! Ask them to give us a spot of light, please.

STAGE-MANAGER: Right you are!

(*He goes off to give the order and a short while after the whole of the right side of the stage, where the* ACTORS *are standing, is lit up by a bright white light. In the meantime the* PROMPTER *has taken his place in his box, switched on his light and spread his script out in front of him.*)

PRODUCER (*clapping his hands*): Come on, let's get started! (*To the* STAGE-MANAGER.) Anyone missing?

STAGE-MANAGER: The Leading Lady.

PRODUCER: As usual! (*Looks at his watch.*) We're ten minutes late already. Make a note, will you, please, to remind me to give her a good talking-to about being so late? It might teach her to get to rehearsals on time in the future.

(*He has scarcely finished his rebuke when the voice of the* LEADING LADY *is heard at the back of the auditorium.*)

LEADING LADY: No, please don't! Here I am! Here I am!

(*She is dressed completely in white, with a large and rather dashing and provocative hat, and is carrying a dainty little lap-dog. She runs down the aisle and hastily climbs up the steps on to the stage.*)

PRODUCER: You've set your heart on always keeping us waiting, haven't you?

LEADING LADY: Forgive me! I hunted everywhere for a taxi so that I should get here on time! But you haven't started yet, anyway. And I don't come on immediately. (*Then, calling the* STAGE-MANAGER *by name, she gives him the lap-dog.*) Please put him in my dressing-room . . . and mind you shut the door!

PRODUCER (*grumblingly*): And she has to bring a dog along too! As if there weren't enough dogs around here! (*He claps his hands again and turns to the* PROMPTER.) Come on now, let's get on with Act II of *The Game As He Played It*. (*He sits down in the armchair.*) Now, ladies and gentlemen, who's on?

(*The* ACTORS AND ACTRESSES *clear away from the front of the stage and go and sit to one side, except for the three who start the scene, and the* LEADING LADY. *She has paid no attention to the* PRODUCER'S *question and has seated herself at one of the little tables.*)

PRODUCER (*to the* LEADING LADY): Ah! So you're in this scene, are you?

LEADING LADY: Me? Oh, no!

PRODUCER (*annoyed*): Then for God's sake get off!

(*And the* LEADING LADY *gets up and goes and sits with the others.*)

PRODUCER (*to the* PROMPTER): Now, let's get started!

PROMPTER (*reading from his script*): "The house of Leone Gala A strange room, half dining-room, half study."

PRODUCER (*turning to the* STAGE MANAGER): We'll use the red set.

STAGE-MANAGER (*making a note on a sheet of paper*): The red set. Right!

PROMPTER (*continuing to read from his script*): "A table laid for a meal and a desk with books and papers. Bookshelves with books on them. Glass-fronted cupboards containing valuable china. A door back leading into Leone's bedroom. A side door left, leading into the kitchen. The main entrance is right."

PRODUCER (*getting up and pointing*): Right! Now listen carefully— over there, the main entrance. And over here, the kitchen. (*Turning to the actor who is to play the part of Socrates.*) You'll make your entrances and exits this side. (*To the* STAGE-MANAGER.) We'll have that green-baize door at the back there . . . and some curtains. (*He goes and sits down again.*)

STAGE-MANAGER (*making a note*): Right you are!

PROMPTER (*reading*): "Scene I. Leone Gala, Guido Venanzi, Filippo, who is called Socrates." (*To the* PRODUCER.) Do I have to read the stage directions as well?

PRODUCER: Yes, yes, of course! I've told you that a hundred times!

PROMPTER (*reading*): "When the curtain rises, Leone Gala, wearing a cook's hat and apron, is busy beating an egg in a basin with a wooden spoon. Filippo, also dressed as a cook, is beating another egg. Guido Venanzi is sitting listening to them."

LEADING MAN (*to the* PRODUCER): Excuse me, but do I really have to wear a cook's hat?

PRODUCER (*irritated by this observation*): So it seems! That's certainly what's written there! (*He points to the script.*)

LEADING MAN: Forgive me for saying so, but it's ridiculous.

PRODUCER (*bounding to his feet in fury*): Ridiculous! Ridiculous! What do you expect me to do if the French haven't got any more good comedies to send us, and we're reduced to putting on plays by Pirandello? And if you can understand *his* plays . . . you're a better man than I am! He deliberately goes out of his way to annoy people, so that by the time the play's through everybody's fed up . . . actors, critics, audience, everybody!

(*The* ACTORS *laugh. Then getting up and going over to the* LEADING MAN, *the* PRODUCER *cries*):

Yes, my dear fellow, a cook's hat! And you beat eggs! And do you think that, having these eggs to beat, you then have nothing more on your hands? Oh, no, not a bit of it. . . . You have to represent the shell of the eggs that you're beating! (*The* ACTORS *start laughing again and begin to make ironical comments among themselves.*)

Shut up! And listen when I'm explaining things! (*Turning again to the* LEADING MAN.) Yes, my dear fellow, the shell . . . or, as you might say, the empty form of reason, without that content of instinct which is blind! You are reason and your wife is instinct, in a game where you play the parts which have been given you. And all the time you're playing your part, you are the self-willed puppet of yourself. Understand?

LEADING MAN (*spreading out his hands*): Me? No!

PRODUCER (*returning to his seat*): Neither do I! However, let's get on with it! It's going to be a wonderful flop, anyway! (*In a confidential tone.*) I suggest you turn to the audience a bit more . . . about three-quarters face. Otherwise, what with the abstruseness of the dialogue, and the audience's not being able to hear you, the whole thing'll go to hell. (*Clapping his hands again.*) Now, come along! *Come along!* Let's get started!

PROMPTER: Excuse me, sir, do you mind if I put the top back on my box? There's a bit of a draught.

PRODUCER: Of course! Go ahead! Go ahead!

(*Meanwhile the* COMMISSIONAIRE *has entered the auditorium. He is wearing a braided cap and having covered the length of the aisle, he*

comes up to the edge of the stage to announce the arrival of the SIX
CHARACTERS to the PRODUCER. They have followed the COM-
MISSIONAIRE into the auditorium and have walked behind him as he
has come up to the stage. They look about them, a little perplexed
and a little dismayed.

In any production of this play it is imperative that the producer
should use every means possible to avoid any confusion between the
SIX CHARACTERS and the ACTORS. The placings of the two groups,
as they will be indicated in the stage-directions once the CHARACTERS
are on the stage, will no doubt help. So, too, will their being lit in
different colours. But the most effective and most suitable method of
distinguishing them that suggests itself, is the use of special masks for
the CHARACTERS, masks specially made from some material which
will not grow limp with perspiration and will at the same time be
light enough to be worn by the actors playing these parts. They should
be cut so as to leave the eyes, the nose and the mouth free. In this way
the deep significance of the play can be brought out. The CHARACTERS
should not, in fact, appear as phantasms, but as created realities,
unchangeable creations of the imagination and, therefore, more real
and more consistent than the ever-changing naturalness of the ACTORS.
The masks will assist in giving the impression of figures constructed
by art, each one fixed immutably in the expression of that sentiment
which is fundamental to it. That is to say in REMORSE for the
FATHER, REVENGE for the STEPDAUGHTER, CONTEMPT for the
SON and SORROW for the MOTHER. Her mask should have wax
tears fixed in the corners of the eyes and coursing down the cheeks,
just like those which are carved and painted in the representations
of the Mater Dolorosa that are to be seen in churches. Her dress,
too, should be of a special material and cut. It should be severely plain,
its folds stiff, giving in fact the appearance of having been carved, and
not of being made of any material that you can just go out and buy or
have cut-out and made up into a dress by any ordinary dressmaker.

The FATHER is a man of about fifty. He is not bald but his reddish
hair is thin at the temples. His moustache is thick and coils over his
still rather youthful-looking mouth, which all too often falls open in
a purposeless, uncertain smile. His complexion is pale and this is
especially noticeable when one has occasion to look at his forehead

which is particularly broad. His blue, oval-shaped eyes are very clear and piercing. He is wearing a dark jacket and light-coloured trousers. At times his manner is all sweetness and light, at others it is hard and harsh.

The MOTHER *appears as a woman crushed and terrified by an intolerable weight of shame and abasement. She is dressed in a modest black and wears a thick crêpe widow's veil. When she lifts her veil she reveals a wax-like face; it is not, however, at all sickly-looking. She keeps her eyes downcast all the time. The* STEPDAUGHTER, *who is eighteen, is defiant, bold, arrogant—almost shamelessly so. She is very beautiful. She, too, is dressed in mourning but carries it with a decided air of showy elegance. She shows contempt for the very timid, dejected, half-frightened manner of her younger brother, a rather grubby and unprepossessing* BOY *of fourteen, who is also dressed in black. On the other hand she displays a very lively tenderness for her small sister, a* LITTLE GIRL *of about four, who is wearing a white frock with a black silk sash round her waist.*

The SON *is a tall young man of twenty-two. He is wearing a mauve coloured overcoat and has a long green scarf twisted round his neck. He appears as if he has stiffened into an attitude of contempt for the* FATHER *and of supercilious indifference towards the* MOTHER.)

COMMISSIONAIRE (*cap in hand*): Excuse me, sir.

PRODUCER (*snapping at him rudely*): Now what's the matter?

COMMISSIONAIRE: There are some people here, sir, asking for you.

(*The* PRODUCER *and the* ACTORS *turn in astonishment and look out into the auditorium.*)

PRODUCER (*furiously*): But I've got a rehearsal on at the moment! And you know quite well that no one's allowed in here while a rehearsal's going on. (*Then addressing the* CHARACTERS.) Who are you? What do you want?

FATHER (*he steps forward, followed by the others, and comes to the foot of one of the flights of steps*): We are here in search of an author.

PRODUCER (*caught between anger and utter astonishment*): In search of an author? Which author?

FATHER: Any author, sir.

PRODUCER: But there's no author here. . . . We're not rehearsing a new play.

STEPDAUGHTER (*vivaciously, as she rushes up the steps*): So much the better! Then so much the better, sir! *We* can be your new play.

ONE OF THE ACTORS (*amidst the lively comments and laughter of the others*): Oh, just listen to her! *Listen* to her!

FATHER (*following the* STEPDAUGHTER *on to the stage*): Yes, but if there isn't any author. . . . (*To the* PRODUCER.) Unless *you'd* like to be the author. . . .

(*Holding the* LITTLE GIRL *by the hand, the* MOTHER, *followed by the* BOY, *climbs up the first few steps leading to the stage and stands there expectantly. The* SON *remains morosely below.*)

PRODUCER: Are you people trying to be funny?

FATHER: No. . . . How can you suggest such a thing? On the contrary, we are bringing you a terrible and grievous drama.

STEPDAUGHTER: And we might make your fortune for you.

PRODUCER: Perhaps you'll do me the kindness of getting out of this theatre! We've got no time to waste on lunatics!

FATHER (*he is wounded by this, but replies in a gentle tone*): Oh. . . . But you know very well, don't you, that life is full of things that are infinitely absurd, things that, for all their impudent absurdity, have no need to masquerade as truth, because they are true.

PRODUCER: What the devil are you talking about?

FATHER: What I'm saying is that reversing the usual order of things, forcing oneself to a contrary way of action, may well be construed as madness. As, for instance, when we create things which have all the appearance of reality in order that they shall look like the realities themselves. But allow me to observe that if this indeed be madness, it is, nonetheless, the sole *raison d'être* of your profession.

(*The* ACTORS *stir indignantly at this.*)

PRODUCER (*getting up and looking him up and down*): Oh, yes? So you think ours is a profession of lunatics, do you?

FATHER: Yes, making what isn't true *seem* true . . . without having to . . . for fun. . . . Isn't it your function to give life on the stage to imaginary characters?

PRODUCER (*immediately, making himself spokesman for the growing anger of his actors*): I should like you to know, my dear sir, that the actor's profession is a most noble one. And although nowadays, with things in the state they are, our playwrights give us stupid comedies to act, and puppets to represent instead of men, I'd have you know that it is our boast that we have given life, here on these very boards, to immortal works! (*The* ACTORS *satisfiedly murmur their approval and applaud the* PRODUCER.)

FATHER (*breaking in and following hard on his argument*): There you are! Oh, that's it exactly! To living beings ... to beings who are more alive than those who breathe and wear clothes! Less real, perhaps, but truer! We're in complete agreement! (*The* ACTORS *look at each other in utter astonishment.*)

PRODUCER: But . . . What on earth! . . . But you said just now . . .

FATHER: No, I said that because of your ... because you shouted at us that you had no time to waste on lunatics ... while nobody can know better than you that nature makes use of the instrument of human fantasy to pursue her work of creation on a higher level.

PRODUCER: True enough! True enough! But where does all this get us?

FATHER: Nowhere. I only wish to show you that one is born into life in so many ways, in so many forms. . . . As a tree, or as a stone; as water or as a butterfly. . . . Or as a woman. And that one can be born a character.

PRODUCER (*ironically, feigning amazement*): And you, together with these other people, were born a character?

FATHER: Exactly. And alive, as you see. (*The* PRODUCER *and the* ACTORS *burst out laughing as if at some huge joke.*) (*Hurt.*) I'm sorry that you laugh like that because, I repeat, we carry within ourselves a terrible and grievous drama, as you can deduce for yourselves from this woman veiled in black.

(*And so saying, he holds out his hand to the* MOTHER *and helps her up the last few steps and, continuing to hold her hand, leads her with a certain tragic solemnity to the other side of the stage, which*

immediately lights up with a fantastic kind of light. The LITTLE
GIRL *and the* BOY *follow their* MOTHER. *Next the* SON *comes up
and goes and stands to one side, in the background. Then the* STEP-
DAUGHTER *follows him on to the stage; she stands downstage,
leaning against the proscenium arch. The* ACTORS *are at first completely taken-aback and then, caught in admiration at this develop-
ment, they burst into applause—just as if they had had a show put
on for their benefit.*)

PRODUCER (*at first utterly astonished and then indignant*): Shut up!
What the . . . ! (*Then turning to the* CHARACTERS.) And you
get out of here! Clear out of here! (*To the* STAGE-MANAGER.)
For God's sake, clear them out!

STAGE-MANAGER (*coming forward, but then stopping as if held back
by some strange dismay*): Go away! Go away!

FATHER (*to the* PRODUCER): No, no! Listen. . . . We. . . .

PRODUCER (*shouting*): I tell you, we've got work to do!

LEADING MAN: You can't go about playing practical jokes like
this. . . .

FATHER (*resolutely coming forward*): I wonder at your incredulity.
Is it perhaps that you're not accustomed to seeing the
characters created by an author leaping to life up here on the
stage, when they come face to face with each other? Or is it,
perhaps, that there's no script there (*he points to the prompt
box*) that contains us?

STEPDAUGHTER (*smiling, she steps towards the* PRODUCER; *then, in a
wheedling voice*): Believe me, sir, we really are six characters . . .
and very, very interesting! But we've been cut adrift.

FATHER (*brushing her aside*): Yes, that's it, we've been cut adrift.
(*And then immediately to the* PRODUCER.) In the sense, you
understand, that the author who created us as living beings,
either couldn't or wouldn't put us materially into the world of
art. And it was truly a crime . . . because he who has the good
fortune to be born a living character may snap his fingers at
Death even. He will never die! Man . . . The writer . . .
The instrument of creation . . . Will die. . . . But what is
created by him will never die. And in order to live eternally
he has not the slightest need of extraordinary gifts or of

accomplishing prodigies. Who was Sancho Panza? Who was Don Abbondio? And yet they live eternally because—living seeds—they had the good fortune to find a fruitful womb—a fantasy which knew how to raise and nourish them, and to make them live through all eternity.

PRODUCER: All this is very, very fine indeed. . . . But what do you want here?

FATHER: We wish to live, sir!

PRODUCER (*ironically*): Through all eternity?

FATHER: No, sir; just for a moment . . . in you.

AN ACTOR: Listen to him! . . . listen to him!

LEADING LADY: They want to live in us!

JUVENILE LEAD (*pointing to the* STEPDAUGHTER): I've no objection . . . so long as I get her.

FATHER: Listen! Listen! The play is in the making. (*To the* PRODUCER.) But if you and your actors are willing, we can settle it all between us without further delay.

PRODUCER (*annoyed*): But what do you want to settle? We don't go in for that sort of concoction here! We put on comedies and dramas here.

FATHER: Exactly! That's the very reason why we came to you.

PRODUCER: And where's the script?

FATHER: It is in us, sir. (*The* ACTORS *laugh*.) The drama is in us. *We* are the drama and we are impatient to act it—so fiercely does our inner passion urge us on.

STEPDAUGHTER (*scornful, treacherous, alluring, with deliberate shamelessness*): My passion. . . . If you only knew! My passion . . . for him!

(*She points to the* FATHER *and makes as if to embrace him, but then bursts into strident laughter.*)

FATHER (*at once, angrily*): You keep out of this for the moment! And please don't laugh like that!

STEPDAUGHTER: Oh . . . mayn't I? Then perhaps *you'll* allow me, ladies and gentlemen. . . . Although it's scarcely two months since my father died . . . just you watch how I can dance and sing!

(*Mischievously she starts to sing Dave Stamper's* "Prends garde à

*Tchou-Thin-Tchou" in the fox-trot or slow one-step version by
François Salabert. She sings the first verse, accompanying it with a
dance.*)

> Les chinois sont un peuple malin,
> De Shangaï à Pékin,
> Ils ont mis des écriteaux partout:
> Prenez garde à Tchou-Thin-Tchou!

(*While she is singing and dancing, the* ACTORS, *and especially the
younger ones, as if attracted by some strange fascination, move towards
her and half raise their hands as though to catch hold of her. She runs
away, and when the* ACTORS *burst into applause, and the* PRODUCER
*rebukes her, she stands where she is, quietly, abstractedly, and as if her
thoughts were far away.*)

ACTORS and ACTRESSES (*laughing and clapping*): Well done! Jolly
good!

PRODUCER (*irately*): Shut up! What do you think this is . . . a
cabaret? (*Then taking the* FATHER *a little to one side, he says with a
certain amount of consternation.*) Tell me something. . . . Is she
mad?

FATHER: What do you mean, mad? It's worse than that!

STEPDAUGHTER (*immediately rushing up to the* PRODUCER): Worse!
Worse! Oh it's something very much worse than that!
Listen! Let's put this drama on at once. . . . Please! Then
you'll see that at a certain moment I . . . when this little darling
here. . . . (*Takes the* LITTLE GIRL *by the hand and brings her over
to the* PRODUCER.) . . . Isn't she a dear? (*Takes her in her arms and
kisses her.*) You little darling! . . . You dear little darling! (*Puts
her down again, adding in a moved tone, almost without wishing to.*)
Well, when God suddenly takes this child away from her poor
mother, and that little imbecile there (*roughly grabbing hold of
the* BOY *by the sleeve and thrusting him forward*) does the stupidest
of all stupid things, like the idiot he is (*pushing him back towards
the* MOTHER) . . . Then you will see me run away. Yes, I shall
run away! And, oh, how I'm longing for that moment to
come! Because after all the very intimate things that have
happened between him and me (*with a horrible wink in the direction of the* FATHER) I can't remain any longer with these people

... having to witness my mother's anguish because of that
queer fish there (*pointing to the* SON). Look at him! Look at
him! See how indifferent, how frigid he is ... because he's
the legitimate son ... *he* is! He despises me, he despises him
(*pointing to the* BOY), he despises that dear little creature. ...
Because we're bastards! Do you understand? ... Because
we're *bastards*! (*She goes up to the* MOTHER *and embraces her.*)
And he doesn't want to recognise this poor woman as his
mother. ... This poor woman ... who is the mother of
us all! He looks down on her as if she were only the mother
of us three bastards! The wretch! (*She says all this very quickly
and very excitedly. She raises her voice at the word 'bastards' and
the final 'wretch' is delivered in a low voice and almost spat out.*)

MOTHER (*to the* PRODUCER, *an infinity of anguish in her voice*): Please,
in the name of these two little children ... I beg you. ...
(*She grows faint and sways on her feet.*) Oh, my God! (*Consternation and bewilderment among the* ACTORS.)

FATHER (*rushing over to support her, accompanied by most of the*
ACTORS): Quick ... a chair. ... A chair for this poor widow!

ACTORS (*rushing over*): Has she fainted? Has she fainted?

PRODUCER: Quick, get a chair ... get a chair!

(*One of the* ACTORS *brings a chair, the others stand around, anxious
to help in any way they can. The* MOTHER *sits on the chair; she
attempts to prevent the* FATHER *from lifting the veil which hides her
face.*)

FATHER: Look at her. ... Look at her. ...

MOTHER: No, No! My God! Stop it, please!

FATHER: Let them see you. (*He lifts her veil.*)

MOTHER (*rising and covering her face with her hands in desperation*):
I beg you, sir, ... Don't let this man carry out his plan! You
must prevent him. ... It's horrible!

PRODUCER (*utterly dumbfounded*): I don't get this at all. ... I
haven't got the slightest idea what you're talking about.
(*To the* FATHER.) Is this lady your wife?

FATHER (*immediately*): Yes, sir, my wife.

PRODUCER: Then how does it come about that she's a widow if
you're still alive?

(*The* ACTORS *find relief for their bewilderment and astonishment in a noisy burst of laughter.*)

FATHER (*wounded, speaking with sharp resentment*): Don't laugh! Don't laugh like that, for pity's sake! It is in this fact that her drama lies. She had another man. Another man who ought to be here.

MOTHER (*with a cry*): No! No!

STEPDAUGHTER: He's got the good luck to be dead. . . . He died two months ago, as I just told you. We're still wearing mourning for him, as you can see.

FATHER: But it's not because he's dead that he's not here. No, he's not here because . . . Look at her! Look at her, please, and you'll understand immediately! Her drama does not lie in the love of two men for whom she, being incapable of love, could feel nothing. . . . Unless, perhaps, it be a little gratitude . . . to him, not to me. She is not a woman. . . . She is a mother. And her drama. . . . And how powerful it is! How powerful it is! . . . Her drama lies entirely, in fact, in these four children. . . . The children of the two men that she had.

MOTHER: Did you say that I had them? Do you dare to say that I *had* these two men . . . to suggest that I wanted them? (*To the* PRODUCER.) It was his doing. He gave him to me! He forced him on me! He forced me. . . . He forced me to go away with that other man!

STEPDAUGHTER (*at once, indignantly*): It's not true!

MOTHER (*startled*): Not true?

STEPDAUGHTER: It's not true! It's not true, I say.

MOTHER: And what can you possibly know about it?

STEPDAUGHTER: It's not true! (*To the* PRODUCER.) Don't believe her! Do you know why she said that? Because of him. (*Pointing to the* SON.) That's why she said it! Because she tortures herself, wears herself out with anguish, because of the indifference of that son of hers. She wants him to believe that if she abandoned him when he was two years old it was because he (*pointing to the* FATHER) forced her to do it.

MOTHER (*forcefully*): He forced me to do it! He forced me, as God is my witness! (*To the* PRODUCER.) Ask him (*pointing to her* HUSBAND) if it's not true! Make him tell my son! She (*pointing to her* DAUGHTER) knows nothing at all about the matter.

STEPDAUGHTER: I know that while my father lived you were always happy. . . . You had a peaceful and contented life together. Deny it if you can!

MOTHER: I don't deny it! No. . . .

STEPDAUGHTER: He was always most loving, always kindness itself towards you. (*To the* BOY, *angrily*.) Isn't it true? Go on. . . . Say it's true! Why don't you speak, you stupid little idiot?

MOTHER: Leave the poor boy alone! Why do you want to make me appear an ungrateful woman? I don't want to say anything against your father. . . . I only said that it wasn't my fault, and that it wasn't just to satisfy my own desires that I left his house and abandoned my son.

FATHER: What she says is true. It was my doing.

(*There is a pause.*)

LEADING MAN (*to the other* ACTORS): My God! What a show!

LEADING LADY: And we're the audience this time!

JUVENILE LEAD: For once in a while.

PRODUCER (*who is beginning to show a lively interest*): Let's listen to this! Let's hear what they've got to say!

(*And saying this he goes down the steps into the auditorium and stands in front of the stage, as if to get an impression of the scene from the audience's point of view.*)

SON (*without moving from where he is, speaking coldly, softly, ironically*): Yes! Listen to the chunk of philosophy you're going to get now! He will tell you all about the Dæmon of Experiment.

FATHER: You're a cynical idiot, as I've told you a hundred times. (*Down to the* PRODUCER.) He mocks me because of this expression that I've discovered in my own defence.

SON (*contemptuously*): Words! Words!

FATHER: Yes! Words! Words! They can always bring consolation to us. . . . To everyone of us. . . . When we're confronted by something for which there's no explanation. . . . When we're face to face with an evil that consumes us. . . .

The consolation of finding a word that tells us nothing, but that brings us peace.

STEPDAUGHTER: And dulls our sense of remorse, too. Yes! That above all!

FATHER: Dulls our sense of remorse? No, that's not true. It wasn't with words alone that I quietened remorse within me.

STEPDAUGHTER: No, you did it with a little money as well. Yes! Oh, yes! with a little money as well! With the hundred lire that he was going to offer me . . . as payment, ladies and gentlemen!

(*A movement of horror on the part of the* ACTORS.)

SON (*contemptuously to his* STEPSISTER): That was vile!

STEPDAUGHTER: Vile? There they were, in a pale blue envelope, on the little mahogany table in the room behind Madame Pace's shop. Madame Pace. . . . One of those *Madames* who pretend to sell *Robes et Manteaux* so that they can attract us poor girls from decent families into their workrooms.

SON: And she's bought the right to tyrannise over the whole lot of us with those hundred lire that he was going to pay her. . . . But by good fortune. . . . And let me emphasise this. . . . He had no reason to pay her anything.

STEPDAUGHTER: Yes, but it was a very near thing! Oh, yes, it was, you know! (*She bursts out laughing.*)

MOTHER (*rising to protest*): For shame! For shame!

STEPDAUGHTER (*immediately*): Shame? No! This is my revenge! I'm trembling with desire. . . . Simply trembling with desire to live that scene! That room. . . . Over here is the shop-window with all the coats in it. . . . And over there the divan, the long mirror and a screen. . . . And in front of the window that little mahogany table. . . . And the pale blue envelope with the hundred lire inside. Yes, I can see it quite clearly! I'd only have to stretch out my hand and I could pick it up! But you gentlemen really ought to turn your backs now, because I'm almost naked. I no longer blush, because he's the one who does the blushing now (*pointing to the* FATHER). But, let me tell you, he was very pale then. . . . Very pale indeed! (*To the* PRODUCER.) You can believe *me*!

PRODUCER: I haven't the vaguest idea what you're talking about!

FATHER: I can well believe it! When you get things hurled at you like that. Put your foot down. . . . And let me speak before you believe all these horrible slanders she's so viciously heaping upon me. . . . Without letting me get a word of explanation in.

STEPDAUGHTER: Ah, but this isn't the place for your long-winded fairy-stories, you know!

FATHER: But I'm not going to. . . . I want to explain things to him!

STEPDAUGHTER: Oh yes . . . I bet you do! You'll explain everything so that it suits you, won't you?

(*At this point the* PRODUCER *comes back on stage to restore order.*)

FATHER: But can't you see that here we have the cause of all the trouble! In the use of words! Each one of us has a whole world of things inside him. . . . And each one us has his own particular world. How can we understand each other if into the words which I speak I put the sense and the value of things as I understand them within myself. . . . While at the same time whoever is listening to them inevitably assumes them to have the sense and value that they have for him. . . . The sense and value that they have in the world that he has within him? We think we understand one another. . . . But we never really do understand! Look at this situation, for example! All my pity, all the pity that I feel for this woman (*pointing to the* MOTHER) *she* sees as the most ferocious cruelty.

MOTHER: But you turned me out of the house!

FATHER: There! Do you hear? I turned her out! She really believed that I was turning her out!

MOTHER: You know how to talk . . . I don't. . . . But believe me (*turning to the* PRODUCER) after he had married me. . . . Goodness knows why! For I was a poor, humble woman. . . .

FATHER: But it was just because of that. . . . It was your humility that I loved in you. I married you for your humility, believing . . . (*He breaks off, for she is making gestures of contradiction. Then, seeing how utterly impossible it is to make her understand him he opens his arms wide in a gesture of despair and turns to the* PRODUCER.) No! . . . You see? She says no! It's terrifying, believe me! It's really terrifying, this deafness (*he taps his forehead*). . . . This mental deafness of hers! Affection. . . . Yes! . . . For her children! But deaf. . . . Mentally deaf. . . . Deaf to the point of desperation.

STEPDAUGHTER: True enough! But now you make him tell us what good all his cleverness has ever done us.

FATHER: If we could only foresee all the ill that can result from the good that we believe we are doing.

(Meanwhile the LEADING LADY, *with ever-increasing fury, has been watching the* LEADING MAN, *who is busy carrying on a flirtation with the* STEPDAUGHTER. *Unable to stand it any longer she now steps forward and says to the* PRODUCER.)

LEADING LADY: Excuse me, but are you going on with the rehearsal?

PRODUCER: Why, of course! Of course! But just at the moment I want to hear what these people have to say!

JUVENILE LEAD: This is really something quite new!

INGENUE: It's most interesting!

LEADING LADY: For those that are interested! (*And she looks meaningly in the direction of the* LEADING MAN.)

PRODUCER (*to the* FATHER): But you'll have to explain everything clearly. (*He goes and sits down.*)

FATHER: Yes. . . . Well. . . . You see . . . I had a poor man working under me. . . . He was my secretary, and devoted to me. . . . Who understood *her* in every way. . . . In everything (*pointing to the* MOTHER). Oh, there wasn't the slightest suspicion of anything wrong. He was a good man. A humble man. . . . Just like her. . . . They were incapable . . . both of them . . . not only of doing evil . . . but even of thinking it!

STEPDAUGHTER: So, instead, he thought about it for them! And then got on with it.

FATHER: It's not true! I thought that what I should be doing would be for their good. . . . And for mine, too. . . . I confess it! Yes, things had come to such a pass that I couldn't say a single word to either of them without their immediately exchanging an understanding look. . . . Without the one's immediately trying to catch the other's eye. . . . For advice as to how to take what I had said. . . . So that I shouldn't get into a bad temper. As you'll readily appreciate it was enough to keep me in a state of continual fury. . . . Of intolerable exasperation!

PRODUCER: But. . . . Forgive my asking. . . . Why didn't you give this secretary of yours the sack?

FATHER: That's exactly what I did do, as a matter of fact. But then I had to watch that poor woman wandering forlornly about the house like some poor lost creature. . . . Like one of those stray animals you take in out of charity.

MOTHER: But . . .

FATHER (*immediately turning on her, as if to forestall what she is about to say*): Your son! You were going to tell him about your son, weren't you?

MOTHER: But first of all he tore my son away from me!

FATHER: Not out of any desire to be cruel though! I took him away so that, by living in the country, in contact with Nature, he might grow up strong and healthy.

STEPDAUGHTER (*pointing to him, ironically*): And just look at him!

FATHER (*immediately*): And is it my fault, too, that he's grown up the way he has? I sent him to a wet-nurse in the country . . . a peasant's wife . . . because my wife didn't seem strong enough to me. . . . Although she came of a humble family, and it was for that reason that I'd married her! Just a whim maybe. . . . But then . . . what was I to do? I've always had this cursed longing for a certain solid moral healthiness.

(*At this the* STEPDAUGHTER *breaks out afresh into noisy laughter.*) Make her stop that noise! I can't stand it!

PRODUCER: Be quiet! Let me hear what he has to say, for God's sake!

(*At the* PRODUCER'S *rebuke she immediately returns to her former attitude. . . . Absorbed and distant, a half-smile on her lips. The* PRODUCER *comes down off the stage again to see how it looks from the auditorium.*)

FATHER: I could no longer stand the sight of that woman near me (*pointing to the* MOTHER). Not so much because of the irritation she caused me . . . the nausea . . . the very real nausea with which she inspired me. . . . But rather because of the pain . . . the pain and the anguish that I was suffering on her account.

MOTHER: And he sent me away!

FATHER: Well provided with everything. . . . To that other man. . . . So that she might be free of me.

MOTHER: And so that he might be free as well!

FATHER: Yes, I admit it. And a great deal of harm came as a result of it. . . . But I meant well. . . . And I did it more for her sake than for my own. I swear it! (*He folds his arms. Then immediately turning to the* MOTHER.) Did I ever lose sight of you? Tell me, did I ever lose sight of you until that fellow took you away suddenly to some other town . . . all unknown to me. . . . Just because he'd got some queer notion into his head about the interest I was showing in you. . . . An interest which was pure, I assure you, sir. . . . Without the slightest suspicion of any ulterior motive about it! I watched the new little family that grew up around her with incredible tenderness. She can testify to that (*he points to the* STEP-DAUGHTER).

STEPDAUGHTER: Oh, I most certainly can! I was such a sweet little girl. . . . Such a sweet little girl, you see. . . . With plaits down to my shoulders . . . and my knickers a little bit longer than my frock. I used to see him standing there by the door of the school as I came out. He came to see how I was growing up. . . .

FATHER: Oh, this is vile! Treacherous! Infamous!

STEPDAUGHTER: Oh, no! What makes you say it's infamous?

FATHER: It's infamous! Infamous! (*Then turning excitedly to the* PRODUCER *he goes on in an explanatory tone.*) After she'd gone away (*pointing to the* MOTHER), my house suddenly seemed empty. She had been a burden on my spirit, but she had filled my house with her presence! Left alone I wandered through the rooms like some lost soul. This boy here (*pointing to the* SON), having been brought up away from home . . . I don't know . . . But . . . But when he returned home he no longer seemed to be my son. With no mother to link him to me, he grew up entirely on his own. . . . A creature apart . . . absorbed in himself . . . with no tie of intellect or affection to bind him to me. And then. . . . And, strange as it may seem, it's the simple truth . . . I became curious about her little family. . . . Gradually I was attracted to this family which had come into being as a result of what I had done. And the thought of it began to fill the emptiness that I felt all around me. I felt a real need . . . a very real need . . . to believe that she was happy, at peace, absorbed in the simple everyday duties of life. I wanted to look on her as being fortunate because she was far removed from the complicated torments of my spirit. And so, to have some proof of this, I used to go and watch that little girl come out of school.

STEPDAUGHTER: I should just say he did! He used to follow me along the street. He would smile at me and when I reached home he'd wave to me . . . like this. I would look at him rather provocatively, opening my eyes wide. I didn't know who he might be. I told my mother about him and she knew at once who it must be. (*The* MOTHER *nods agreement.*) At first she didn't want to let me go to school again. . . . And she kept me away for several days. And when I did go back, I saw him waiting for me at the door again . . . looking so ridiculous . . . with a brown paper bag in his hand. He came up to me and patted me. . . . And then he took a lovely large straw hat out of the bag . . . with lots of lovely little roses on it. . . . And all for me.

PRODUCER: This is a bit off the point, you know.

SON (*contemptuously*): Yes. . . . Literature! Literature!

FATHER: Literature indeed! This is life! Passion!

PRODUCER: It may be. But you certainly can't act this sort of stuff!

FATHER: I agree with you. Because all this is only leading up to the main action. I'm not suggesting that this part should be acted. And as a matter of fact, as you can quite well see, she (*pointing to the* STEPDAUGHTER) is no longer that little girl with plaits down to her shoulders. . . .

STEPDAUGHTER: . . . and her knickers a little bit longer than her frock!

FATHER: It is now that the drama comes! Something new, something complex. . . .

STEPDAUGHTER (*coming forward, her voice gloomy, fierce*): As soon as my father died. . . .

FATHER (*at once, not giving her a chance to continue*): . . . they fell into the most wretched poverty! They came back here. . . . And because of her stupidity (*pointing to the* MOTHER) I didn't know a thing about it. It's true enough that she can hardly write her own name. . . . But she might have got her daughter or that boy to write and tell me that they were in need!

MOTHER: Now tell me, sir, how was I to know that this was how he'd feel?

FATHER: That's exactly where you went wrong, in never having got to know how I felt about anything.

MOTHER: After so many years away from him. . . . And after all that had happened. . . .

FATHER: And is it my fault that that fellow took you away from here as he did? (*Turning to the* PRODUCER.) I tell you, they disappeared overnight. . . . He'd found some sort of a job away from here . . . I couldn't trace them at all. . . . So, of necessity, my interest in them dwindled. And this was how it was for quite a number of years. The drama broke out, unforeseen and violent in its intensity, when they returned. . . . When I was impelled by the demands of my miserable flesh, which is still alive with desire. . . . Oh, the wretchedness, the unutterable wretchedness of the man who's alone and who detests the vileness of casual affairs! When he's not old enough to do without a woman, and not really young enough to be able to go and look for one without feeling a sense of shame. Wretchedness, did I say? It's horrible! It's horrible! Because no woman is any longer capable of giving him love. And when he realises this, he ought to do without. . . . Yes, yes, I know! . . . Each one of us, when he appears before his fellow men, is clothed with a certain dignity. But deep down inside himself he knows what unconfessable

things go on in the secrecy of his own heart. We give way . . .
we give way to temptation. . . . Only to rise up again immediately, filled with a great eagerness to re-establish our
dignity in all its solid entirety. . . . Just as if it were a tomb-
stone on some grave in which we had buried, in which we
had hidden from our eyes, every sign, and the very memory
itself of our shame. And everyone is just like that! Only
there are some of us who lack the courage to talk about
certain things.

STEPDAUGHTER: They've got the courage to do them,
though. . . . All of them!

FATHER: Yes, all of them! But only in secret! And that's why
it needs so much more courage to talk about them! A man's
only got to mention these things, and the words have hardly
left his lips before he's been labelled a cynic. And all the time
it's not true. He's just like everybody else. . . . In fact he's
better than they are, because he's not afraid to reveal with the
light of his intelligence that red blush of shame which is
inherent in human bestiality. . . . That shame to which bestial
man closes his eyes, in order not to see it. And woman. . . .
Yes, woman. . . . What kind of a being is she? She looks at
you, tantalisingly, invitingly. You take her in your arms!
And no sooner is she clasped firmly in your arms than she
shuts her eyes. It is the sign of her mission, the sign by which
she says to man, "Blind yourself, for I am blind."

STEPDAUGHTER: And what about when she no longer shuts her
eyes? When she no longer feels the need to hide her blushing
shame from herself by closing her eyes? When she sees
instead . . . dry-eyed and dispassionate . . . the blushing shame
of man, who has blinded himself without love? Oh, what
disgust, what unutterable disgust, does she feel then for all
these intellectual complications, for all this philosophy which
reveals the beast in man and then tries to save him, tries to
excuse him . . . I just can't stand here and listen to him!
Because when a man is obliged to 'simplify' life bestially like
that—when he throws overboard every vestige of 'humanity',
every chaste desire, every pure feeling. . . . All sense of

idealism, of duty, of modesty and of shame. . . . Then nothing is more contemptible, infuriating and revoltingly nauseating than their maudlin remorse. . . . Those crocodile tears!

PRODUCER: Now let's get back to the point! Let's get to the point! This is just a lot of beating the about bush!

FATHER: Very well. But a fact is like a sack. . . . When it's empty it won't stand up. And in order to make it stand up you must first of all pour into it all the reasons and all the feelings which have caused it to exist. I couldn't possibly be expected to know that when that man died and they returned here in such utter poverty, she (*pointing to the* MOTHER) would go out to work as a dress-maker in order to support the children. . . . Nor that, of all people, she'd gone to work for that . . . for Madame Pace.

STEPDAUGHTER: Who's a high-class dress-maker, if you ladies and gentlemen would really like to know. On the surface she does work for only the best sort of people. But she arranges things so that these fine ladies act as a screen . . . without prejudice to the others . . . who are only so-so.

MOTHER: Believe me, it never entered my head for one moment that that old hag gave me work because she had her eye on my daughter. . . .

STEPDAUGHTER: Poor Mummy! Do you know what that woman used to do when I took her back the work that my mother had done? She would point out to me how the material had been ruined by giving it to my mother to sew. . . . Oh, she'd grumble about this! And she'd grumble about that! And so, you understand, I had to pay for it. . . . And all the time this poor creature thought she was sacrificing herself for me and for those two children, as she sat up all night sewing away at work for Madame Pace. (*Gestures and exclamations of indignation from the* ACTORS.)

PRODUCER (*immediately*): And it was there, one day, that you met . . .

STEPDAUGHTER (*pointing to the* FATHER): . . . him! Yes, him! An old client! Now there's a scene for you to put on! Absolutely superb!

FATHER: With her ... the Mother ... arriving. ...

STEPDAUGHTER (*immediately*, *treacherously*): ... almost in time!

FATHER (*a cry*): No! In time! In time! Fortunately I recognised her in time! And I took them all back home with me! Now you can imagine what the situation is like for both of us. She, just as you see her. ... And I, no longer able to look her in the face.

STEPDAUGHTER: It's utterly ridiculous! How can I possibly be expected, after all that, to be a modest young miss ... well-bred and virtuous ... in accordance with his confounded aspirations for a "solid moral healthiness"?

FATHER: My drama lies entirely in this one thing. ... In my being conscious that each one of us believes himself to be a single person. But it's not true. ... Each one of us is many persons. ... Many persons ... according to all the possibilities of being that there are within us. ... With some people we are one person. ... With others we are somebody quite different. ... And all the time we are under the illusion of always being one and the same person for everybody. ... We believe that we are always this one person in whatever it is we may be doing. But it's not true! It's not true! And we see this very clearly when by some tragic chance we are, as it were, caught up whilst in the middle of doing something and find ourselves suspended in mid-air. And then we perceive that all of us was not in what we were doing, and that it would, therefore, be an atrocious injustice to us to judge us by that action alone. ... To keep us suspended like that. ... To keep us in a pillory ... throughout all existence ... as if our whole life were completely summed up in that one deed. Now do you understand the treachery of this girl? She surprised me somewhere where I shouldn't have been ... and doing something that I shouldn't have been doing with her. ... She surprised an aspect of me that should never have existed for her. And now she is trying to attach to me a reality such as I could never have expected I should have to assume for her. ... The reality that lies in one fleeting, shameful moment of my life. And this, this above all, is what I feel most strongly about. And as you can see, the drama acquires a tremendous value from this concept. Then there's the position of the others. . . . His . . . (*pointing to the* SON).

SON (*shrugging his shoulders scornfully*): Leave me alone! I've got nothing to do with all this!

FATHER: What do you mean . . . you've got nothing to do with all this?

SON: I've got nothing to do with it. . . . And I don't want to have anything to do with it, because, as you quite well know, I wasn't meant to be mixed up in all this with the rest of you!

STEPDAUGHTER: Common, that's what we are! And he's a fine gentleman! But, as you may have noticed, every now and again I fix him with a contemptuous look, and he lowers his eyes. . . . Because he knows the harm he's done me!

SON (*scarcely looking at her*): I?

STEPDAUGHTER: Yes, you! You! It's all your fault that I became a prostitute! (*A movement of horror from the* ACTORS.) Did you or did you not deny us, by the attitude you adopted—I won't say the intimacy of your home—but even that mere hospitality which makes guests feel at their ease? We were invaders who had come to disturb the kingdom of your legitimacy. I should just like you (*this to the* PRODUCER) to be present at certain little scenes that took place between him and me. He says that I tyrannised over everybody. . . . But it was just because of the way that he behaved that I took advantage of the thing that he calls 'vile'. . . . Why I exploited the reason for my coming into his house with my mother. . . . Who is his mother as well! And I went into that house as mistress of it!

SON (*slowly coming forward*): It's all very easy for them. . . . It's fine sport. . . . All of them ganging-up against me. But just imagine the position of a son whose fate it is one fine day, while he's sitting quietly at home, to see arriving an impudent and brazen young woman who asks for his father—and heaven knows what her business is with him! Later he sees her come back, as brazen as ever, bringing that little girl with her. And finally he sees her treating his father—without knowing in the least why—in a very equivocal and very much to-the-point manner . . . asking him for money, in a tone of voice which leads you to suppose that he must give it to her. . . . Must give it to her, because he has every obligation to do so. . . .

FATHER: As indeed I have! It's an obligation I owe your mother!

SON: How should I know that? When had I ever seen or even heard of her? Then one day I see her arrive with *her* (*pointing to the* STEPDAUGHTER) together with that boy and the little girl. And they say to me, "This is *your* mother, too, you know." Little by little I begin to understand. . . . Largely as a result of the way she goes on (*pointing to the* STEPDAUGHTER *again*). . . . Why it is that they've come to live with us. . . . So suddenly. . . . So unexpectedly. . . . What I feel, what I experience, I neither wish, nor am able, to express. I wouldn't even wish to confess it to myself. No action, therefore, can be hoped for from me in this affair. Believe me, I am a dramatically unrealised character . . . and I do not feel the least bit at ease in their company. So please leave me out of it!

FATHER: What! But it's just because you're like that. . . .

SON (*in violent exasperation*): And what do you know about it? How do you know what I'm like? When have you ever bothered yourself about me?

FATHER: I admit it! I admit it! But isn't that a dramatic situation in itself? This aloofness of yours, which is so cruel to me and to your mother. . . . Your mother who returns home and sees you almost for the first time. . . . You're so grown up that she doesn't recognise you, but she knows that you're her son. (*Pointing to the* MOTHER *and addressing the* PRODUCER.) There, look! She's crying!

STEPDAUGHTER (*angrily, stamping her foot*): Like the fool she is!

FATHER (*pointing to the* STEPDAUGHTER): She can't stand him! (*Then returning to the subject of the* SON.) He says he's got nothing to do with all this, when, as a matter of fact, almost the whole action hinges on him. Look at that little boy. . . . See how he clings to his mother all the time, frightened and humiliated. . . . And it's *his* fault that he's like that! Perhaps his position is the most painful of all. . . . More than any of them he feels himself to be an outsider. And so the poor little chap feels mortified, humiliated at being taken into my home . . . out of charity, as it were. (*Confidentially.*) He's just like his father. Humble. . . . Doesn't say a word. . . .

PRODUCER: I don't think it's a good idea to have him in. You've no idea what a nuisance boys are on the stage.

FATHER: Oh, . . . but he won't be a nuisance for long. . . . He disappears almost immediately. And the little girl, too. . . . In fact, she's the first to go.

PRODUCER: This is excellent! I assure you I find this all very interesting. . . . Very interesting indeed! I can see we've got the makings of a pretty good play here.

STEPDAUGHTER (*trying to butt in*): When you've got a character like me!

FATHER (*pushing her to one side in his anxiety to hear what decision the PRODUCER has come to*): You be quiet!

PRODUCER (*continuing, heedless of the interruption*): And it's certainly something new. . . . Ye-es! . . .

FATHER: Absolutely brand new!

PRODUCER: You had a nerve, though, I must say. . . . Coming here and chucking the idea at me like that. . . .

FATHER: Well, you understand, born as we are for the stage. . . .

PRODUCER: Are you amateur actors?

FATHER: No . . . I say that we're born for the stage because . . .

PRODUCER: Oh, don't try and come that one with me! You're an old hand at this game.

FATHER: No. I only act as much as anyone acts the part that he sets himself to perform, or the part that he is given in life. And in me it is passion itself, as you can see, that always becomes a little theatrical of its own accord . . . as it does in everyone . . . once it becomes exalted.

PRODUCER: Oh well, that as may be! That as may be! . . . But you do understand, without an author . . . I could give you the address of somebody who'd . . .

FATHER: No! . . . Look here. . . . You be the author!

PRODUCER: Me? What the devil are you talking about?

FATHER: Yes, you! You! Why not?

PRODUCER: Because I've never written anything in my life! That's why not!

FATHER: Then why not try your hand at it now? There's nothing to it. Everybody's doing it! And your job's made all the easier for you because we are here, all of us, alive before you. . . .

PRODUCER: That's not enough!

FATHER: Not enough? When you see us live our drama. . . .

PRODUCER: Yes! Yes! But we'll still need somebody to write the play.

FATHER: No. . . . Someone to take it down possibly, while we act it out, scene by scene. It'll be quite sufficient if we make a rough sketch of it first and then have a run through.

PRODUCER (*climbing back on to the stage, tempted by this*): H'm! . . . You almost succeed in tempting me. . . . H'm! It would be rather fun! We could certainly have a shot at it.

FATHER: Of course! Oh, you'll see what wonderful scenes 'll emerge! I can tell you what they are here and now.

PRODUCER: You tempt me. . . . You tempt me. . . . Let's have a go at it! . . . Come with me into my office. (*Turning to the* ACTORS.) You can have a few minutes' break. . . . But don't go too far away. I want you all back again in about a quarter of an hour or twenty minutes. (*To the* FATHER.) Well, let's see what we can make of it! We might get something really extraordinary out of it. . . .

FATHER: There's no *might* about it! They'd better come along too, don't you think? (*Pointing to the other* CHARACTERS.)

PRODUCER: Yes, bring 'em along! Bring 'em along! (*Starts going off and then turns back to the* ACTORS.) Now remember, don't be late back! You've got a quarter of an hour!

(*The* PRODUCER *and the* SIX CHARACTERS *cross the stage and disappear. The* ACTORS *remain looking at one another in astonishment.*)

LEADING MAN: Is he serious? What's he going to do?

JUVENILE LEAD: This is utter madness!

A THIRD ACTOR: Does he expect us to knock up a play in five minutes?

JUVENILE LEAD: Yes . . . like the actors in the old Commedia dell' Arte.

LEADING LADY: Well, if he thinks that I'm going to have anything to do with fun and games of that sort. . . .

INGENUE: And you certainly don't catch me joining in!

A FOURTH ACTOR: I should like to know who those people are. (*He is alluding to the* CHARACTERS.)

THIRD ACTOR: Who do you think they're likely to be? They're probably escaped lunatics. . . . Or crooks!

JUVENILE LEAD: And does he really take what they say seriously?

INGENUE: Vanity! That's what it is. . . . The vanity of appearing as an author!

LEADING MAN: It's absolutely unheard of! If the stage has come to this. . . .

A FIFTH ACTOR: I'm rather enjoying it!

THIRD ACTOR: Oh, well! After all, we shall have the pleasure of seeing what comes of it all!

And talking among themselves in this way the ACTORS *leave the stage. Some go out through the door back, some go in the direction of the dressing-rooms. The curtain remains up.*

The performance is suspended for twenty minutes.

The call-bells ring, warning the audience that the performance is about to be resumed.

The ACTORS, *the* STAGE-MANAGER, *the* FOREMAN *of the stage crew, the* PROMPTER *and the* PROPERTY MAN *reassemble on stage. Some come from the dressing-rooms, some through the door back, some even from the auditorium. The* PRODUCER *enters from his office accompanied by the* SIX CHARACTERS.

The houselights are extinguished and the stage lighting is as before.

PRODUCER: Now come on, ladies and gentlemen! Are we all here? Let me have your attention please! Now let's make a start! (*Then calls the* FOREMAN.)

FOREMAN: Yes, sir?

PRODUCER: Set the stage for the parlour scene. A couple of flats and a door will do. As quickly as you can!

(*The* FOREMAN *runs off at once to carry out this order and is setting the stage as directed whilst the* PRODUCER *is making his arrangements with the* STAGE-MANAGER, *the* PROPERTY MAN, *the* PROMPTER *and the* ACTORS. *The flats he has set up are painted in pink and gold stripes.*)

PRODUCER (*to* PROPERTY MAN): Just have a look, please, and see if we've got some sort of sofa or divan in the props room.

PROPERTY MAN: There's the green one, sir.

STEPDAUGHTER: No, no, green won't do! It was yellow . . yellow flowered plush. . . . A huge thing . . . and most comfortable.

PROPERTY MAN: Well, we haven't got anything like that.

PRODUCER: It doesn't matter! Give me what there is!

STEPDAUGHTER: What do you mean, it doesn't matter? Madame Pace's famous sofa!

PRODUCER: We only want it for this run-through. Please don't interfere. (*To the* STAGE-MANAGER.) Oh, and see if we've got a shop-window . . . something rather long and narrowish is what we want.

STEPDAUGHTER: And a little table . . . the little mahogany table for the pale blue envelope!

STAGE-MANAGER (*to* PRODUCER): There's that little one. . . . You know, the gold-painted one.

PRODUCER: That'll do fine! Shove it on!

FATHER: You need a long mirror.

STEPDAUGHTER: And the screen!   I must have a screen, please. . . . Else how can I manage?

STAGE-MANAGER: Don't you worry, Miss! We've got masses of them!

PRODUCER (*to the* STEPDAUGHTER): And some clothes-hangers and so on, h'm?

STEPDAUGHTER: Oh, yes, lots!

PRODUCER (*to the* STAGE-MANAGER): See how many we've got and get somebody to bring them up.

STAGE-MANAGER: Right you are, sir, I'll see to it!

(*The* STAGE-MANAGER *goes off about his business and while the* PRODUCER *is talking to the* PROMPTER *and later to the* CHARACTERS *and* ACTORS, *he gets the stage hands to bring up the furniture and properties and proceeds to arrange them in what he thinks is the best sort of order.*)

PRODUCER (*to the* PROMPTER): Now if you'll get into position while they're setting the stage. . . . Look, here's an outline of the thing. . . . Act I . . . Act II . . . (*he holds out some sheets of paper to him*). But you'll really have to excel yourself this time.

PROMPTER: You mean, take it down in shorthand?

PRODUCER (*pleasantly surprised*): Oh, good man! Can you do shorthand?

PROMPTER: I mayn't know much about prompting, but shorthand. . . .

PRODUCER: Better and better. (*Turning to a* STAGE-HAND.) Go and get some paper out of my room. . . . A large wadge. . . . As much as you can find!

(*The* STAGE-HAND *hurries off and returns shortly with a thick wadge of paper which he gives to the* PROMPTER.)

PRODUCER (*to the* PROMPTER): Follow the scenes closely as we play them and try and fix the lines . . . or at least the most important ones. (*Then, turning to the* ACTORS.) Right, ladies and gentlemen, clear the stage, please! No, come over this side (*he waves them over to his left*) . . . and pay careful attention to what goes on.

LEADING LADY: Excuse me, but we . . .

PRODUCER (*forestalling what she is going to say*): There won't be any improvising to do, don't you worry!

LEADING MAN: What *do* we have to do, then?

PRODUCER: Nothing. For the moment all you've got to do is to stay over there and watch what happens. You'll get your parts later. Just now we're going to have a rehearsal . . . or as much of one as we can in the circumstances! And *they'll* be doing the rehearsing (*he points to the* CHARACTERS).

FATHER (*in consternation, as if he had tumbled from the clouds into the midst of all the confusion on stage*): We are? But, excuse me, in what way will it be a rehearsal?

PRODUCER: Well . . . a rehearsal . . . a rehearsal for *their* benefit. (*He points to the* ACTORS.)

FATHER: But if we're the characters . . .

PRODUCER: Just so, "the characters". But it's not characters that act here. It's actors who do the acting here. The characters remain there, in the script (*he points to the prompt-box*). . . . When there is a script!

FATHER: Precisely! And since there is no script and you have the good fortune to have the characters here alive before your very eyes. . . .

PRODUCER: Oh, this is wonderful! Do you want to do everything on your own? Act . . . present yourselves to the public?

FATHER: Yes, just as we are.

PRODUCER: And let me tell you you'd make a wonderful sight!

LEADING MAN: And what use should we be then?

PRODUCER: You're not going to pretend that you can act, are you? Why, it's enough to make a cat laugh. . . . (*And as a matter of fact, the* ACTORS *burst out laughing.*) There you are, you see, they're laughing at the idea! (*Then, remembering.*) But, to the point! I must tell you what your parts are. That's not so very difficult. They pretty well cast themselves. (*To the* SECOND ACTRESS.) You, the Mother. (*To the* FATHER.) We'll have to find a name for her.

FATHER: Amalia.

PRODUCER: But that's your wife's name. We can hardly call her by her real name.

FATHER: And why not, when that's her name? But, perhaps, if it has to be that lady . . . (*a slight gesture to indicate the* SECOND ACTRESS) I see *her* (*pointing to the* MOTHER) as Amalia. But do as you like. . . . (*His confusion grows.*) I don't know what to say to you. . . . I'm already beginning. . . . I don't know how to express it . . . to hear my own words ringing false . . . as if they had another sound from the one I had meant to give them. . . .

PRODUCER: Now don't you worry about that! Don't you worry

about it at all! We'll think about how to get the right tone
of voice. And as for the name. . . . If you want it to be Amalia,
Amalia it shall be. Or we'll find some other name. Just for
the present we'll refer to the characters in this way. (*To the*
JUVENILE LEAD.) You, the Son. . . (*To the* LEADING LADY.)
And you'll play the Stepdaughter, of course. . . .

STEPDAUGHTER (*excitedly*): What! What did you say? That
woman there. . . . Me! (*She bursts out laughing.*)

PRODUCER (*angrily*): And what's making you laugh?

LEADING LADY (*indignantly*): Nobody has ever dared to laugh at
me before! Either you treat me with respect or I'm walking
out!

STEPDAUGHTER: Oh, no, forgive me! I wasn't laughing at you.

PRODUCER (*to* STEPDAUGHTER): You should feel yourself
honoured to be played by . . .

LEADING LADY (*immediately, disdainfully*): . . . "that woman
there."

STEPDAUGHTER: But my remark wasn't meant as a criticism of
you . . . I was thinking about myself. . . . Because I can't see
myself in you at all. I don't know how to . . . you're not a
bit like me!

FATHER: Yes, that's the point I wanted to make! Look . . . all
that we express. . . .

PRODUCER: What do you mean . . . *all that you express*? Do you
think that this whatever-it-is that you express is something
you've got inside you? Not a bit of it.

FATHER: Why . . . aren't even the things we express our own?

PRODUCER: Of course they aren't! The things that you express
become material here for the actors, who give it body and
form, voice and gesture. And, let me tell you, my actors have
given expression to much loftier material than this. This stuff
of yours is so trivial that, believe me, if it comes off on the
stage, the credit will all be due to my actors.

FATHER: I don't dare to contradict you! But please believe me
when I tell you that we . . . who have these bodies . . . these
features. . . . Who are as you see us now. . . . We are suffering
horribly. . . .

PRODUCER (*cutting in impatiently*): . . . But the make-up will remedy all that. . . . At least as far as your faces are concerned!

FATHER: Perhaps. . . . But what about our voices? . . . What about our gestures? . . .

PRODUCER: Now, look here! You, as yourself, just cannot exist here! Here there's an actor who'll play you. And let that be an end to all this argument!

FATHER: I understand. . . . And now I think I see why our author didn't wish to put us on the stage after all. . . . He saw us as we are. . . . Alive. . . . He saw us as living beings. . . . I don't want to offend your actors. . . . Heaven forbid that I should! . . . But I think that seeing myself acted now . . . by I don't know whom . . .

LEADING MAN (*rising with some dignity and coming over, followed by a laughing group of young actresses*): By me, if you have no objection.

FATHER (*humbly, mellifluously*): I am deeply honoured, sir. (*He bows.*) But. . . . Well. . . . I think that however much of his art this gentleman puts into absorbing me into himself. . . . However much he wills it. . . . (*He becomes confused.*)

LEADING MAN: Go on! Go on! (*The actresses laugh.*)

FATHER: Well, I should say that the performance he'll give. . . . Even if he makes himself up to look as much like me as he can. . . . I should say that with his figure . . . (*All the* ACTORS *laugh*) . . . it will be difficult for it to be a performance of me . . . of me as I really am. It will rather be . . . leaving aside the question of his appearance. . . . It will be how he interprets what I am . . . how he sees me. . . . If he sees me as anything at all. . . . And not as I, deep down within myself, feel myself to be. And it certainly seems to me that whoever is called upon to criticise us will have to take this into account.

PRODUCER: So you're already thinking about what the critics will say, are you? And here am I, still trying to get the play straight! The critics can say what they like. We'd be much better occupied in thinking about getting the play on. . . . If we can. (*Stepping out of the group and looking around him.*) Now, come on, let's make a start! Is everything ready? (*To the*

ACTORS *and* CHARACTERS.) Come on, don't clutter up the place! Let me see how it looks! (*He comes down from the stage.*) And now, don't let's lose any more time! (*To the* STEPDAUGHTER.) Do you think the set looks all right?

STEPDAUGHTER: To be perfectly honest, I just don't recognise it at all!

PRODUCER: Good Lord, you surely didn't hope that we were going to reconstruct that room behind Madame Pace's shop here on the stage, did you? (*To the* FATHER.) You did tell me it had flowered wallpaper, didn't you?

FATHER: Yes, white.

PRODUCER: Well, it's not white—and it's got stripes on it—but it'll have to do! As for the furniture, I think we've more or less got everything we need. Bring that little table down here a bit! (*The* STAGE HANDS *do so. Then he says to the* PROPERTY MAN.) Now, will you go and get an envelope. . . . A pale blue one if you can. . . . And give it to that gentleman. (*He points to the* FATHER.)

PROPERTY MAN: The kind you put letters in?

PRODUCER and FATHER: Yes, the kind you put letters in!

PROPERTY MAN: Yes, sir! At once, sir! (*Exit.*)

PRODUCER: Now, come on! First scene—the young lady. (*The* LEADING LADY *comes forward.*) No! No! Wait a moment! I said the young lady! (*Pointing to the* STEPDAUGHTER.) You stay there and watch. . . .

STEPDAUGHTER (*immediately adding*): . . . how I make it live!

LEADING LADY (*resentfully*): I'll know how to make it live, don't you worry, once I get started!

PRODUCER (*with his hands to his head*): Ladies and gentlemen, don't let's have any arguing! Please! Right! Now . . . The first scene is between the young lady and Madame Pace. Oh! (*He looks around rather helplessly and then comes back on stage.*) What about this Madame Pace?

FATHER: She's not with us, sir.

PRODUCER: And what do we do about her?

FATHER: But she's alive! She's alive too!

PRODUCER: Yes, yes! But where is she?

FATHER: If you'll just allow me to have a word with your people. . . . (*Turning to the* ACTRESSES.) I wonder if you ladies would do me the kindness of lending me your hats for a moment.

THE ACTRESSES (*a chorus . . . half-laughing, half-surprised.*): What? Our hats?
What did he say?
Why?
Listen to the man!

PRODUCER: What are you going to do with the women's hats? (*The* ACTORS *laugh.*)

FATHER: Oh, nothing . . . I just want to put them on these pegs for a moment. And perhaps one of you ladies would be so kind as to take off your coat, too.

THE ACTORS (*laughter and surprise in their voices*): Their coats as well?
And after that?
The man must be mad!

ONE OR TWO OF THE ACTRESSES (*surprise and laughter in their voices*): But why?
Only our coats?

FATHER: So that I can hang them here. . . . Just for a moment or so. . . . Please do me this favour. Will you?

THE ACTRESSES (*they take off their hats. One or two take off their coats as well, all laughing the while. They go over and hang the coats here and there on the pegs and hangers*):
And why not?
Here you are!
This really is funny!
Do we have to put them on show?

FATHER: Precisely. . . . You have to put them on show. . . . Like this!

PRODUCER: Is one allowed to know what you're up to?

FATHER: Why, yes. If we set the stage better, who knows whether she may not be attracted by the objects of her trade and perhaps appear among us. . . . (*He invites them to look towards the door at the back of the stage.*) Look! Look!

(*The door opens and* MADAME PACE *comes in and takes a few steps forward. She is an enormously fat old harridan of a woman, wearing a pompous carrot-coloured tow wig with a red rose stuck into one side of it, in the Spanish manner. She is heavily made up and dressed with clumsy elegance in a stylish red silk dress. In one hand she carries an ostrich feather fan; the other hand is raised and a lighted cigarette is poised between two fingers. Immediately they see this apparition, the* ACTORS *and the* PRODUCER *bound off the stage with howls of fear, hurling themselves down the steps into the auditorium and making as if to dash up the aisle. The* STEPDAUGHTER, *however, rushes humbly up to* MADAME PACE, *as if greeting her mistress.*)

STEPDAUGHTER (*rushing up to her*): Here she is! Here she is!

FATHER (*beaming*): It's Madame Pace! What did I tell you? Here she is!

PRODUCER (*his first surprise overcome, he is now indignant*): What sort of a game do you call this?

LEADING MAN:		Hang it all, what's going on?
JUVENILE LEAD:	*Almost at the same moment and all speaking at once.*	Where did *she* spring from?
INGENUE:		They were keeping her in reserve!
LEADING LADY:		So it's back to the music hall and conjuring tricks, is it?

FATHER (*dominating the protesting voices*): One moment, please! Why should you wish to destroy this prodigy of reality, which was born, which was evoked, attracted and formed by this scene itself? . . . A reality which has more right to live here than you have. . . . Because it is so very much more alive than you are. . . . Why do you want to spoil it all, just because of some niggling, vulgar convention of truth? . . . Which of you actresses will be playing the part of Madame Pace? Well, *that* woman *is* Madame Pace! Grant me at least that the actress who plays her will be less true than she is. . . . For *she* is Madame Pace in person! Look! My daughter recognised her and went up to her at once. Now, watch this scene! Just watch it! (*Hesitantly the* PRODUCER *and the* ACTORS *climb back on to the stage. But while the* ACTORS *have been protesting and the* FATHER *has been replying to them, the scene between the* STEP-DAUGHTER *and* MADAME PACE *has begun. It is carried on in an undertone, very quietly—naturally in fact—in a manner that would be quite impossible on the stage. When the* ACTORS *obey the* FATHER'S *demand that they shall watch what is happening, they see that* MADAME PACE *has already put her hand under the* STEPDAUGHTER'S *chin to raise her head and is talking to her. Hearing her speak in a completely unintelligible manner they are held for a moment. But almost immediately their attention flags.*)

PRODUCER: Well?

LEADING MAN: But what's she saying?

LEADING LADY: We can't hear a thing!

JUVENILE LEAD: Speak up! Louder!

STEPDAUGHTER (*she leaves* MADAME PACE *and comes down to the group of* ACTORS. MADAME PACE *smiles—a priceless smile*): Did you say, 'Louder?' What do you mean, 'Louder?' What we're talking about is scarcely the sort of thing to be shouted from the roof-tops. I was able to yell it out just now so that I could shame *him* (*pointing to the* FATHER). . . . So that I could have my revenge! But it's quite another matter for Madame Pace. . . . It would mean prison for her.

PRODUCER: Indeed? So that's how it is, is it? But let me tell you something, my dear young lady. . . . Here in the theatre you've got to make yourself heard! The way you're doing this bit at the moment even those of us who're on stage can't hear you! Just imagine what it'll be like with an audience out front. This scene's got to be got over. And anyway there's nothing to prevent you from speaking up when you're on together. . . . We shan't be here to listen to you. . . . We're only here now because it's a rehearsal. Pretend you're alone in the room behind the shop, where nobody can hear you.

(*The* STEPDAUGHTER *elegantly, charmingly—and with a mischievous smile—wags her finger two or three times in disagreement.*

PRODUCER: What do you mean, 'No?'

STEPDAUGHTER (*in a mysterious whisper*): There's someone who'll hear us if *she* (*pointing to* MADAME PACE) speaks up.

PRODUCER (*in utter consternation*): Do you mean to say that there's somebody else who's going to burst in on us? (*The* ACTORS *make as if to dive off the stage again.*)

FATHER: No! No! They're alluding to me. I have to be there, waiting behind the door. . . . And Madame Pace knows it. So, if you'll excuse me, I'll go. . . . So that I'm all ready to make my entrance. (*He starts off towards the back of the stage.*)

PRODUCER (*stopping him*): No! No! Wait a moment! When you're here you have to respect the conventions of the theatre! Before you get ready to go on to that bit. . . .

STEPDAUGHTER: No! Let's get on with it at once! At once! I'm dying with desire, I tell you . . . to live this scene. . . . To live it! If he wants to get on with it right away, I'm more than ready!

PRODUCER (*shouting*): But first of all, the scene between you and her (*pointing to* MADAME PACE) has got to be got over! Do you understand?

STEPDAUGHTER: Oh, my God! She's just been telling me what *you* already know. . . . That once again my mother's work has been badly done. . . . That the dress is spoilt. . . . And that I must be patient if she is to go on helping us in our misfortune.

MADAME PACE (*stepping forward, a grand air of importance about her*): But, yes, señor, porque I not want to make profit . . . to take advantàge. . . .

PRODUCER (*more than a touch of terror in his voice*): What? Does she speak like that?

(*The* ACTORS *burst into noisy laughter.*)

STEPDAUGHTER (*laughing too*): Yes, she speaks like that, half in English, half in Spanish. . . . It's most comical.

MADAME PACE: Ah, no, it does not to me seem good manners that you laugh of me when I . . . force myself to . . . hablar, as I can, English, señor!

PRODUCER: Indeed, no! It's very wrong of us! You speak like that! Yes, speak like that, Madame! It'll bring the house down! We couldn't ask for anything better. It'll bring a little comic relief into the crudity of the situation. Yes, you talk like that! It's absolutely wonderful!

STEPDAUGHTER: Wonderful! And why not? When you hear a certain sort of suggestion made to you in a lingo like that. . . . There's not much doubt about what your answer's going to be. . . . Because it almost seems like a joke. You feel inclined to laugh when you hear there's an 'old señor' who wants to 'amuse himself with me'. An 'old señor', eh, Madame?

MADAME PACE: Not so very old. . . . Not quite so young, yes? And if he does not please to you. . . . Well, he has . . . *prudencia*.

MOTHER (*absorbed as they are in the scene the* ACTORS *have been paying no attention to her. Now, to their amazement and consternation, she leaps up and attacks* MADAME PACE. *At her cry they jump, then hasten smilingly to restrain her, for she, meanwhile, has snatched off* MADAME PACE'S *wig and has thrown it to the ground*): You old devil! You old witch! You murderess! Oh, my daughter!

STEPDAUGHTER (*rushing over to restrain her* MOTHER): No, Mummy, no! Please!

FATHER (*rushing over at the same time*): Calm yourself, my dear! Just be calm! Now . . . come and sit down again!

MOTHER: Take that woman out of my sight, then!

(*In the general excitement the* PRODUCER, *too, has rushed over and the* STEPDAUGHTER *now turns to him.*)

STEPDAUGHTER: It's impossible for my mother to remain here!

FATHER (*to the* PRODUCER): They can't be here together. That's why, when we first came, that woman wasn't with us. If they're on at the same time the whole thing is inevitably given away in advance.

PRODUCER: It doesn't matter! It doesn't matter a bit! This is only a first run-through. . . . Just to give us a rough idea how it goes. Everything'll come in useful . . . I can sort out the bits and pieces later. . . . I'll make something out of it, even if it is all jumbled up. (*Turning to the* MOTHER *and leading her back to her chair.*) Now, please be calm, and sit down here, nice and quietly.

(*Meanwhile the* STEPDAUGHTER *has gone down centre stage again. She turns to* MADAME PACE.)

STEPDAUGHTER: Go on, Madame, go on!

MADAME PACE (*offended*): Ah, no thank you! Here I do not do nothing more with your mother present!

STEPDAUGHTER: Now, come on! Show in the 'old señor' who wants to 'amuse himself with me'. (*Turning imperiously on the rest.*) Yes, this scene has got to be played. So let's get on with it! (*To* MADAME PACE.) You can go!

MADAME PACE: Ah, I am going . . . I am going. . . . Most assuredly I am going! (*Exit furiously, ramming her wig back on and glowering at the* ACTORS, *who mockingly applaud her.*)

STEPDAUGHTER (*to the* FATHER): And now you make your entrance! There's no need for you to go out and come in again! Come over here! Pretend that you've already entered! Now, I'm standing here modestly, my eyes on the ground Come on! Speak up! Say, 'Good afternoon, Miss,' in that special tone of voice . . . you know. . . . Like somebody who's just come in from the street.

PRODUCER (*by this time he is down off the stage*): Listen to her! Are you running this rehearsal, or am I? (*To the* FATHER, *who is looking perplexed and undecided.*) Go on, do as she tells you! Go to the back of the stage. . . . Don't exit! . . . And then come forward again.

(*The* FATHER *does as he is told. He is troubled and very pale. But as he approaches from the back of the stage he smiles, already absorbed in the reality of his created life. He smiles as if the drama which is about to break upon him is as yet unknown to him. The* ACTORS *become intent on the scene which is beginning.*)

PRODUCER (*whispering quickly to the* PROMPTER, *who has taken up his position*): Get ready to write now!

THE SCENE

FATHER (*coming forward, a new note in his voice*): Good afternoon, Miss.

STEPDAUGHTER (*her head bowed, speaking with restrained disgust*): Good afternoon!

FATHER (*studying her a little, looking up into her face from under the brim of her hat (which almost hides it), and perceiving that she is very young, exclaims, almost to himself, a little out of complacency, a little, too, from the fear of compromising himself in a risky adventure*): H'm! But. . . . M'm. . . . This won't be the first time, will it? The first time that you've been here?

STEPDAUGHTER (*as before*): No, sir.

FATHER: You've been here before? (*And since the* STEPDAUGHTER *nods in affirmation.*) More than once? (*He waits a little while for her reply, resumes his study of her, again looking up into her face from under the brim of her hat, smiles and then says.*) Then . . . well . . . it shouldn't any longer be so. . . . May I take off your hat?

STEPDAUGHTER (*immediately forestalling him, unable to restrain her disgust*): No, sir, I'll take it off myself! (*Convulsed, she hurriedly takes it off.*)

(*The* MOTHER *is on tenterhooks throughout. The* TWO CHILDREN *cling to their* MOTHER *and they, she and the* SON *form a group on the side opposite the* ACTORS, *watching the scene. The* MOTHER *follows the words and the actions of the* STEPDAUGHTER *and the* FATHER *with varying expressions of sorrow, of indignation, of anxiety and of horror; from time to time she hides her face in her hands and sobs.*)

MOTHER: Oh, my God! My God!

FATHER (*he remains for a moment as if turned to stone by this sob. Then he resumes in the same tone of voice as before*): Here, let me take it. I'll hang it up for you. (*He takes the hat from her hands.*) But such a charming, such a dear little head really ought to have a much smarter hat than this! Would you like to come and help me choose one from among these hats of Madame's? Will you?

INGENUE (*breaking in*): Oh, I say! Those are *our* hats!

PRODUCER (*at once, furiously*): For God's sake, shut up! Don't try to be funny! We're doing our best to rehearse this scene, in case you weren't aware of the fact! (*Turning to* STEPDAUGHTER.) Go on from where you left off, please.

STEPDAUGHTER (*continuing*): No thank you, sir.

FATHER: Come now, don't say no. Do say you'll accept it. . . . Just to please me. I shall be most upset if you won't. . . .

Look, here are some rather nice ones. And then it would please Madame. She puts them out on show on purpose, you know.

STEPDAUGHTER: No . . . listen! I couldn't wear it.

FATHER: You're thinking perhaps about what they'll say when you come home wearing a new hat? Well now, shall I tell you what to do? Shall I tell you what to say when you get home?

STEPDAUGHTER (*quickly—she is at the end of her tether*): No, it's not that! I couldn't wear it because I'm . . . As you see. . . . You should have noticed already . . . (*indicating her black dress*).

FATHER: That you're in mourning! Of course. . . . Oh, forgive me! Of course! Oh, I beg your pardon! Believe me. . . . I'm most profoundly sorry. . . .

STEPDAUGHTER (*summoning all her strength and forcing herself to conquer her contempt, her indignation and her nausea*): Stop! Please don't say any more! I really ought to be thanking you. There's no need for you to feel so very sorry or upset! Please don't give another thought to what I said! I, too, you understand. . . . (*Tries hard to smile and adds.*) I really must forget that I'm dressed like this!

PRODUCER (*interrupting them; he climbs back on to the stage and turns to the* PROMPTER): Hold it! Stop a minute! Don't write that down. Leave out that last bit. (*Turning to the* FATHER *and the* STEPDAUGHTER.) It's going very well! Very well indeed! (*Then to the* FATHER.) And then you go on as we arranged. (*To the* ACTORS.) Rather delightful, that bit where he offers her the hat, don't you think?

STEPDAUGHTER: Ah, but the best bit's coming now! Why aren't we going on?

PRODUCER: Now be patient, please! Just for a little while! (*Turning to the* ACTORS.) Of course it'll have to be treated rather lightly. . . .

LEADING MAN: . . . M'm . . . and put over slickly. . . .

LEADING LADY: Of course! There's nothing difficult about it at all. (*To the* LEADING MAN.) Shall we try it now?

LEADING MAN: As far as I'm . . . I'll go and get ready for my entrance. (*Exit to take up his position outside the door back.*)

PRODUCER (*to the* LEADING LADY): Now, look. . . . The scene between you and Madame Pace is finished. I'll get down to writing it up properly afterwards. You're standing. . . . Where are you going?

LEADING LADY: Just a moment! I want to put my hat back on. . . . (*Goes over, takes her hat down and puts it on.*)

PRODUCER: Good! Now you stand here. With your head bowed down a bit.

STEPDAUGHTER (*amused*): But she's not dressed in black!

LEADING LADY: I *shall* be dressed in black. . . . And much more becomingly than you are!

PRODUCER (*to the* STEPDAUGHTER): Shut up . . . please! And watch! You'll learn something. (*Claps his hands.*) Now come on! Let's get going! Entrance! (*He goes down from the stage again to see how it looks from out front. The door back opens and the* LEADING MAN *steps forward. He has the lively, raffish, self-possessed air of an elderly gallant. The playing of this scene by the* ACTORS *will appear from the very first words as something completely different from what was played before, without its having, even in the slightest degree, the air of a parody. It should appear rather as if the scene has been touched up. Quite naturally the* FATHER *and the* STEPDAUGHTER, *not being able to recognise themselves at all in the* LEADING LADY *and* LEADING MAN, *yet hearing them deliver the very words they used, react in a variety of ways, now with a gesture, now with a smile, with open protest even, to the impression they receive. They are surprised, lost in wonder, in suffering . . . as we shall see. The* PROMPTER'S *voice is clearly heard throughout the scene.*)

LEADING MAN: Good afternoon, Miss!

FATHER (*immediately, unable to restrain himself*): No! No! (*And the* STEPDAUGHTER, *seeing the* LEADING MAN *enter in this way, bursts out laughing.*)

PRODUCER (*infuriated*): Shut up! And once and for all . . . Stop that laughing! We shan't get anywhere if we go on like this!

STEPDAUGHTER (*moving away from the proscenium*): Forgive me . . .

but I couldn't help laughing! This lady (*pointing to the* LEADING LADY) stands just where you put her, without budging an inch . . . But if she's meant to be me. . . . I can assure you that if I heard anybody saying 'Good afternoon' to me in that way and in that tone of voice I'd burst out laughing. . . . So I had to, you see.

FATHER (*coming forward a little, too*): Yes, that's it exactly. . . . His manner. . . . The tone of voice. . . .

PRODUCER: To hell with your manner and your tone of voice! Just stand to one side, if you don't mind, and let me get a look at this rehearsal.

LEADING MAN (*coming forward*): Now if I've got to play an old fellow who's coming into a house of rather doubtful character. . . .

PRODUCER: Oh, don't take any notice of him! Now, *please*! Start again, please! It was going very nicely. (*There is a pause—he is clearly waiting for the* LEADING MAN *to begin again.*) Well?

LEADING MAN: Good afternoon, Miss.

LEADING LADY: Good afternoon!

LEADING MAN (*repeating the* FATHER's *move—that is, looking up into the* LEADING LADY's *face from under the brim of her hat; but then expressing very clearly first his satisfaction and then his fear*): M'm . . . this won't be the first time, I hope. . . .

FATHER (*unable to resist the temptation to correct him*): Not 'hope'— 'will it?', 'will it?'

PRODUCER: You say 'will it?' . . . It's a question.

LEADING MAN (*pointing to the* PROMPTER): I'm sure he said, 'hope.'

PRODUCER: Well, it's all one! 'Hope' or whatever it was! Go on, please! Go on. . . . Oh, there was one thing . . . I think perhaps it ought not to be quite so heavy. . . . Hold on, I'll show you what I mean. Watch me. . . . (*Comes back on to the stage. Then, making his entrance, he proceeds to play the part.*) Good afternoon, Miss.

LEADING LADY: Good afternoon. . . .

PRODUCER: M'm. . . . (*Turning to the* LEADING MAN *to impress on him the way he has looked up at the* LEADING LADY *from under the brim of her hat.*) Surprise, fear and satisfaction. (*Then turning back to the* LEADING LADY.) It won't be the first time, will it, that you've been here? (*Turning again to the* LEADING MAN *enquiringly.*) Is that clear? (*To the* LEADING LADY.) And then you say, 'No, sir.' (*To the* LEADING MAN.) There you are. . . . It wants to be a little more . . . what shall I say? . . . A little more *flexible*. A little more *souple*! (*He goes down from the stage again.*)

LEADING LADY: No, sir. . . .

LEADING MAN: You've been here before? More than once?

PRODUCER: Wait a minute! You must let her (*pointing to the* LEADING LADY) get her nod in first. You've been here before? (*The* LEADING LADY *lifts her head a little, closing her eyes painfully as if in disgust and then when the* PRODUCER *says* Down, *nods twice.*)

STEPDAUGHTER (*unable to restrain herself*): Oh, my God! (*And immediately she puts her hand over her mouth to stifle her laughter.*)

PRODUCER (*turning*): What's the matter?

STEPDAUGHTER (*immediately*): Nothing! Nothing!

PRODUCER (*to the* LEADING MAN): It's your cue. . . . Carry straight on.

LEADING MAN: More than once? Well then . . . Come along. . . . May I take off your hat?
(*The* LEADING MAN *says this last line in such a tone of voice and accompanies it with such a gesture that the* STEPDAUGHTER, *who has remained with her hands over her mouth, can no longer restrain herself. She tries desperately to prevent herself from laughing but a noisy burst of laughter comes irresistibly through her fingers.*)

LEADING LADY (*turning indignantly*): I'm not going to stand here and be made a fool of by that woman!

LEADING MAN: And neither am I. Let's pack the whole thing in.

PRODUCER (*shouting at the* STEPDAUGHTER): Once and for all, will you shut up!

STEPDAUGHTER: Yes. . . . Forgive me, please! . . . Forgive me!

PRODUCER: The trouble with you is that you've got no manners! You go too far!

FATHER (*trying to intervene*): Yes, sir, you're quite right! Quite right! But you must forgive her. . . .

PRODUCER (*climbing back on to the stage*): What do you want me to forgive? It's absolutely disgusting the way she's behaving!

FATHER: Yes. . . . But . . . Oh, believe me . . . Believe me, it has such a strange effect. . . .

PRODUCER: Strange! How do you mean, 'Strange'? What's so strange about it?

FATHER: You see, sir, I admire . . . I admire your actors. . . . That gentleman there (*pointing to the* LEADING MAN) and that lady (*pointing to the* LEADING LADY) . . . But . . . Well . . . The truth is . . . They're certainly not us!

PRODUCER: I should hope not! How do you expect them to be *you* if they're actors?

FATHER: Just so, actors. And they play our parts well, both of them. But when they act . . . To us they seem to be doing something quite different. They want to be the same . . . And all the time they just aren't.

PRODUCER: But how aren't they the same? What are they then?

FATHER: Something that becomes theirs . . . And no longer ours.

PRODUCER: But that's inevitable! I've told you that already.

FATHER: Yes, I understand . . . I understand that. . . .

PRODUCER: Well then, let's hear no more on the subject! (*Turning to the* ACTORS.) We'll run through it later by ourselves in the usual way. I've always had a strong aversion to holding rehearsals with the author present. He's never satisfied! (*Turning to the* FATHER *and the* STEPDAUGHTER.) Now, come on, let's get on with it! And let's see if we can have no more laughing! (*To the* STEPDAUGHTER.)

STEPDAUGHTER: Oh, I shan't laugh any more! I promise you! My big bit's coming now. . . . Just you wait and see!

PRODUCER: Well, then. . . . When you say, 'Please don't give another thought to what I said! I, too, you understand. . . .' (*Turning to the* FATHER.) You come in at once with, 'I understand! I understand!' and immediately ask . . .

STEPDAUGHTER (*interrupting him*): What? What does he ask?

PRODUCER: . . . why you're in mourning.

STEPDAUGHTER: Oh, no! That's not it at all! Listen! When I told him that I mustn't think about my being in mourning, do you know what his answer was? 'Well, then, let's take this little frock off at once, shall we?'

PRODUCER: That would be wonderful! Wonderful! That *would* bring the house down!

STEPDAUGHTER: But it's the truth!

PRODUCER: But what's the truth got to do with it? Acting's what *we're* here for! Truth's all very fine . . . But only up to a point.

STEPDAUGHTER: And what do you want then?

PRODUCER: You'll see! You'll see. Leave everything to me.

STEPDAUGHTER: No, I won't! What you'd like to do, no doubt, is to concoct a romantic, sentimental little affair out of my disgust, out of all the reasons, each more cruel, each viler than the other, why I am this sort of woman, why I am what I am! An affair with him! He asks me why I'm in mourning and I reply with tears in my eyes that my father died only two months ago. No! No! He must say what he said then, 'Well, then, let's take this little frock off at once, shall we?' And I . . . my heart still grieving for my father's death. . . . I went behind there . . . Do you understand? . . . There, behind that screen! And then, my fingers trembling with shame and disgust, I took off my frock, undid my brassière. . . .

PRODUCER (*running his hands through his hair*): For God's sake! What on earth are you saying, girl?

STEPDAUGHTER (*crying out excitedly*): The truth! The truth!

PRODUCER: Yes, it probably is the truth! I'm not denying it! And I understand . . . I fully appreciate all your horror. But you must realise that we simply can't put this kind of thing on the stage.

STEPDAUGHTER: Oh, you can't, can't you? If that's how things are, thanks very much! I'm going!

PRODUCER: No! No! Look here! . . .

STEPDAUGHTER: I'm going! I'm not stopping here! You worked it all out together, didn't you? . . . The pair of you. . . . You and him. . . . When you were in there. . . . You worked

out what was going to be possible on the stage. Oh, thanks
very much! I understand! He wants to jump to the bit where
he presents his spiritual torments! (*This is said harshly*.) But
I want to present my own drama! *Mine! Mine!*

PRODUCER (*his shoulders shaking with annoyance*): Ah! There we
have it! *Your* drama! Look here . . . you'll have to forgive me
for telling you this . . . but there isn't only your part to be
considered! Each of the others has his drama, too. (*He
points to the* FATHER.) He has his and your Mother has hers.
You can't have one character coming along like this, becoming
too prominent, invading the stage in and out of season and
overshadowing all the rest. All the characters must be con-
tained within one harmonious picture, and presenting only
what it is proper to present. I'm very well aware that everyone
carries a complete life within himself and that he wants to
put it before the whole world. But it's here that we run into
difficulties: how are we to bring out only just so much as is
absolutely necessary? . . . And at the same time, of course, to
take into account all the other characters. . . . And yet in that
small fragment we have to be able to hint at all the rest of the
secret life of that character. Ah, it would be all very pleasant
if each character could have a nice little monologue. . . . Or
without making any bones about it, give a lecture, in which he
could tell his audience what's bubbling and boiling away
inside him. (*His tone is good-humoured, conciliatory*.) You must
restrain yourself. And believe me, it's in your own interest,
too. Because all this fury . . . this exasperation and this
disgust . . . They make a bad impression. Especially when . . .
And pardon me for mentioning this. . . . You yourself have
confessed that you'd had other men there at Madame Pace's
before him. . . . And more than once!

STEPDAUGHTER (*bowing her head. She pauses a moment in recollection
and then, a deeper note in her voice*): That is true! But you must
remember that those other men mean *him* for me, just as much
as he himself does!

PRODUCER (*uncomprehending*): What? The other men mean *him*?
What do you mean?

STEPDAUGHTER: Isn't it true that in the case of someone who's gone wrong, the person who was responsible for the first fault is responsible for all the faults which follow? And in my case, he is responsible. . . . Has been ever since before I was born. Look at him, and see if it isn't true!

PRODUCER: Very well, then! And does this terrible weight of remorse that is resting on his spirit seem so slight a thing to you? Give him the chance of acting it!

STEPDAUGHTER: How? How can he act all his 'noble' remorse, all his 'moral' torments, if you want to spare him all the horror of one day finding in his arms. . . . After he had asked her to take off her frock . . . her grief still undulled by time. . . . The horror of finding in his arms that child. . . . A woman now, and a fallen woman already. . . . That child whom he used to go and watch as she came out of school? (*She says these last words in a voice trembling with emotion. The* MOTHER, *hearing her talk like this, is overcome by distress which expresses itself at first in stifled sobs. Finally she breaks out into a fit of bitter crying. Everyone is deeply moved. There is a long pause.*)

STEPDAUGHTER (*gravely and resolutely, as soon as the* MOTHER *shows signs of becoming a little quieter*): At the moment we are here, unknown as yet by the public. Tomorrow you will present us as you wish. . . . Making up your play in your own way. But would you really like to see our drama? To see it flash into life as it did in reality?

PRODUCER: Why, of course! I couldn't ask for anything better, so that from now on I can use as much as possible of it.

STEPDAUGHTER: Well, then, ask my Mother to leave us.

MOTHER (*rising, her quiet weeping changed to a sharp cry*): No! No! Don't you allow them to do it! Don't allow them to do it!

PRODUCER: But it's only so that I can see how it goes.

MOTHER: I can't bear it! I can't bear it!

PRODUCER: But since it's already happened, I don't understand!

MOTHER: No, it's happening now! It happens all the time! My torment is no pretence, sir. I am alive and I am present always. . . . At every moment of my torment. . . . A torment which is for ever renewing itself. Always alive and always present. But those two children there. . . . Have you heard them say a single word? They can no longer speak! They cling to me still. . . . In order to keep my torment living and present! But for themselves they no longer exist! They no longer exist! And she (*pointing to the* STEPDAUGHTER) . . . She has run away. . . . Run away from me and is lost. . . . Lost! . . . And if I see her here before me it is for this reason and for this reason alone. . . . To renew at all times. . . . Forever. . . . To bring before me again, present and living, the anguish that I have suffered on her account too.

FATHER (*solemnly*): The eternal moment, as I told you, sir. She (*he points to the* STEPDAUGHTER) . . . She is here in order to fix me. . . . To hold me suspended throughout all eternity. . . . In the pillory of that one fleeting shameful moment in my life. She cannot renounce her rôle. . . . And you, sir, cannot really spare me my agony.

PRODUCER: Quite so, but I didn't say that I wouldn't present it. As a matter of fact it'll form the basis of the first act. . . . Up to the point where she surprises you (*pointing to the* MOTHER).

FATHER: That is right. Because it is my sentence. All our passion. . . . All our suffering. . . . Which must culminate in *her* cry (*pointing to the* MOTHER).

STEPDAUGHTER: I can still hear it ringing in my ears! That cry sent me mad! You can play me just as you like. . . . It doesn't matter. Dressed, if you like, provided that I can have my arms bare at least. . . . Just my arms bare. . . . Because, you see, standing there . . . (*She goes up to the* FATHER *and rests her head on his chest.*) With my head resting on his chest like this . . . and with my arms round his neck . . . I could see a vein throbbing away in my arm. And then . . . Just as if that pulsing vein alone gave me a sense of horror . . . I shut my eyes tight and buried my head in his chest. (*Turning towards the* MOTHER.) Scream, Mummy! Scream! (*She buries her head in the* FATHER'S *chest and, raising her shoulders as if in order not to hear the cry, adds in a voice stifled with torment.*) Scream, as you screamed then!

MOTHER (*rushing upon them to separate them*): No! No! She's my daughter! (*And having torn her daughter away.*) You brute! You brute! She's my daughter! Can't you see that she's my daughter?

PRODUCER (*retreating at the cry right up to the footlights, amid the general dismay of the* ACTORS): Excellent! Excellent! And then . . . Curtain! Curtain!

FATHER (*rushing over to him convulsively*): Yes, because that's how it really happened!

PRODUCER (*quite convinced, admiration in his voice*): Oh, yes, we must have the curtain there. . . . That cry and then . . . Curtain! Curtain!

(*At the repeated shouts of the* PRODUCER *the* STAGE HAND *on the curtain lets it down, leaving the* PRODUCER *and the* FATHER *between it and the footlights.*)

PRODUCER (*looking up, his arms raised*): Oh, the damned fool! I say, 'Curtain' . . . Meaning that I want the act to end there. . . . And he really does go and bring the curtain down. (*To the* FATHER, *lifting up a corner of the curtain.*) Oh, yes! That's absolutely wonderful! Very good indeed! That'll get them! There's no *if or but* about it. . . . That line and then . . . *Curtain!* We've got something in that first act . . . or I'm a Dutchman! (*Disappears through the curtain with the* FATHER.)

When the curtain goes up again the audience sees that the STAGE-HANDS *have dismantled the previous set and put on in its place a small garden fountain. On one side of the stage the* ACTORS *are sitting in a row, and on the other side, the* CHARACTERS. *The* PRODUCER *is standing in a meditative attitude in the middle of the stage with his hand clenched over his mouth. There is a brief pause; then:*

PRODUCER (*with a shrug of his shoulders*): Oh, well! . . . Let's get on with Act II! Now if you'll only leave it all to me, as we agreed, everything'll sort itself out.

STEPDAUGHTER: This is where we make our entry into his house . . . (*Pointing to the* FATHER.) In spite of him! (*Pointing to the* SON.)

PRODUCER (*out of patience*): Yes, yes! But leave it to me, I tell you!

STEPDAUGHTER: Well. . . . So long as it's made quite clear that it was against his wishes.

MOTHER (*from the corner, shaking her head*): For all the good that's come of it. . . .

STEPDAUGHTER (*turning to her quickly*): That doesn't matter! The more harm that it's done us, the more remorse for him!

PRODUCER (*impatiently*): I understand all that! I'll take it all into account! Don't you worry about it!

MOTHER (*a supplicant note in her voice*): But I do beg you, sir . . . To set my conscience at rest. . . . To make it quite plain that I tried in every way I could to . . .

STEPDAUGHTER (*interrupting contemptuously and continuing her* MOTHER's *speech*): . . . to pacify me, to persuade me not to get my own back. . . . (*To the* PRODUCER.) Go on . . . do what she asks you! Give her that satisfaction. . . . Because she's quite right, you know! I'm enjoying myself no end, because . . . Well, just look. . . . The meeker she is, the more she tries to wriggle her way into his heart, the more he holds himself aloof, the more distant he becomes. I can't think why she bothers!

PRODUCER: Are we going to get started on the second act or are we not?

STEPDAUGHTER: I won't say another word! But, you know, it won't be possible to play it all in the garden, as you suggested.

PRODUCER: Why not?

STEPDAUGHTER: Because he (*pointing to the* SON *again*) shuts himself up in his room all the time. . . . Holding himself aloof. . . . And, what's more, there's all the boy's part. . . . Poor bewildered little devil. . . . As I told you, all that takes place indoors.

PRODUCER: I know all about that! On the other hand you do understand that we can hardly stick up notices telling the

audience what the scene is. . . . *Or* change the set three or
four times in one act.

LEADING MAN: They used to in the good old days.

PRODUCER: Oh, yes. . . . When the intelligence of the audience
was about up to the level of that little girl's there. . . .

LEADING LADY: And it does make it easier to get the sense of
illusion.

FATHER (*immediately, rising*): Illusion, did you say? For Heaven's
sake, please don't use the word illusion! Please don't use
that word. . . . It's a particularly cruel one for us!

PRODUCER (*astounded*): And why's that?

FATHER: It's cruel! Cruel! You should have known that!

PRODUCER: What ought we to say then? We were referring to
the illusion that we have to create on this stage . . . for the
audience. . . .

LEADING MAN: . . . with our acting. . . .

PRODUCER: . . . the illusion of a reality!

FATHER: I understand, sir. But you . . . Perhaps you can't
understand us. Forgive me! Because . . . you see . . . for you
and for your actors, all this is only . . . and quite rightly so. . . .
All this is only a game.

LEADING LADY (*indignantly interrupting him*): What do you mean,
a game? We're not children! We're serious actors!

FATHER: I don't deny it! And in fact, in using the term, I was
referring to your art which must, as this gentleman has said,
create a perfect illusion of reality.

PRODUCER: Precisely!

FATHER: Now just consider the fact that we (*pointing quickly to
himself and to the other* FIVE CHARACTERS) as ourselves, have no
other reality outside this illusion!

PRODUCER (*in utter astonishment, looking round at his actors who show
the same bewildered amazement*): And what does all that mean?

FATHER (*the ghost of a smile on his face. There is a brief pause while
he looks at them all*): As I said. . . . What other reality should we
have? What for you is an illusion that you have to create, for
us, on the other hand, is our sole reality. The only reality we
know. (*There is a short pause. Then he takes a step or two towards*

the PRODUCER *and adds.*) But it's not only true in our case,
you know. Just think it over. (*He looks into his eyes.*) Can you
tell me who you are? (*And he stands there pointing his index
finger at him.*)

PRODUCER (*disturbed, a half-smile on his lips*): What? Who am I?
I'm myself!

FATHER: And suppose I were to tell you that that wasn't true?
Suppose I told you that you were me? . . .

PRODUCER: I should say that you were mad! (*The* ACTORS
laugh.)

FATHER: You're quite right to laugh, because here everything's
a game. (*To the* PRODUCER.) And you can object, therefore,
that it's only in fun that that gentleman (*pointing to the* LEADING
MAN) who is *himself* must be *me* who, on the contrary, am
myself. . . . That is, *the person you see here.* There, you see.
I've caught you in a trap! (*The* ACTORS *laugh again.*)

PRODUCER (*annoyed*): But you said all this not ten minutes ago!
Do we have to go over all that again?

FATHER: No. As a matter of fact that wasn't what I intended.
I should like to invite you to abandon this game. . . . (*Looking
at the* LEADING LADY *as if to forestall what she will say.*) Your
art! Your art! . . . The game that it is customary for you and
your actors to play here in this theatre. And once again I ask
you in all seriousness. . . . Who are you?

PRODUCER (*turning to the* ACTORS *in utter amazement, an amazement not unmixed with irritation*): What a cheek the fellow has!
A man who calls himself a character comes here and asks
me who I am!

FATHER (*with dignity, but in no way haughtily*): A character, sir,
may always ask a man who he is. Because a character has
a life which is truly his, marked with his own special
characteristics. . . . And as a result he is always somebody!
Whilst a man. . . . And I'm not speaking of you personally
at the moment. . . . Man in general . . . Can quite well be
nobody.

PRODUCER: That as may be! But you're asking *me* these
questions. Me, do you understand? The Producer! The boss!

FATHER (*softly, with gentle humility*): But only in order to know if you, you as you really are now, are seeing yourself as, for instance, after all the time that has gone by, you see yourself as you were at some point in the past. . . . With all the illusions that you had then . . . with everything . . . all the things you had deep down inside you . . . everything that made up your external world . . . everything as it appeared to you then . . . and as it *was*, as it was in reality for you then! Well . . thinking back on those illusions which you no longer have . . . on all those things that no longer *seem* to be what they *were* once upon a time . . . don't you feel that . . . I won't say these boards. . . . No! . . . That the very earth itself is slipping away from under your feet, when you reflect that in the same way this *you* that you now feel yourself to be . . . all your reality as it is today . . . is destined to seem an illusion tomorrow?

PRODUCER (*not having understood much of all this, and somewhat taken aback by this specious argument*): Well? And where does all this get us, anyway?

FATHER: Nowhere. I only wanted to make you see that if we (*again pointing to himself and to the other* CHARACTERS) have no reality outside the world of illusion, it would be as well if you mistrusted your own reality. . . . The reality that you breathe and touch today. . . . Because like the reality of yesterday, it is fated to reveal itself as a mere illusion tomorrow.

PRODUCER (*deciding to make fun of him*): Oh, excellent! And so you'd say that you and this play of yours that you've been putting on for my benefit are more real than I am?

FATHER (*with the utmost seriousness*): Oh, without a doubt.

PRODUCER: Really?

FATHER: I thought that you'd understood that right from the very beginning.

PRODUCER: More real than I am.

FATHER: If your reality can change from one day to the next. . . .

PRODUCER: But everybody knows that it can change like that! It's always changing. . . . Just like everybody else's!

FATHER (*with a cry*): No, ours doesn't change! You see. . . .
That's the difference between us! Our reality doesn't
change. . . . It can't change. . . . It can never be in any way
different from what it is. . . . Because it is already fixed. . . .
Just as it is. . . . For ever! For ever it is *this* reality. . . . It's
terrible! . . . This immutable reality. . . . It should make you
shudder to come near us!

PRODUCER (*quickly, suddenly struck by an idea. He moves over and
stands squarely in front of him*): I should like to know, however,
when anyone ever saw a character step out of his part and
begin a long dissertation on it like the one you've just been
making. . . . Expounding it. . . . Explaining it. . . . Can you
tell me? . . . I've never seen it happen before!

FATHER: You have never seen it happen before because authors
usually hide the details of their work of creation. Once the
characters are alive. . . . Once they are standing truly alive
before their author. . . . He does nothing but follow the words
and gestures that they suggest to him. . . . And he must want
them to be what they themselves want to be. For woe betide
him if he doesn't do what they wish him to do! When a
character is born he immediately acquires such an indepen-
dence. . . . Even of his own author. . . . That everyone can
imagine him in a whole host of situations in which his author
never thought of placing him. . . . They can even imagine his
acquiring, sometimes, a significance that the author never
dreamt of giving him.

PRODUCER: Yes. . . . I know all that!

FATHER: Well, then, why are you so astonished at seeing us?
Just imagine what a misfortune it is for a character to be born
alive. . . . Created by the imagination of an author who afterwards sought to deny him life. . . . Now tell me whether a
character who has been left unrealised in this way. . . . Living,
yet without a life. . . . Whether this character hasn't the right
to do what we are doing now. . . . Here and now. . . . For your
benefit? . . . After we had spent . . . Oh, such ages, believe
me! . . . Doing it for his benefit . . . Trying to persuade him,
trying to urge him to realise us. . . . First of all I would present

myself to him. . . . Then she would . . . (*pointing to the* STEP-
DAUGHTER). . . . And then her poor Mother. . . .

STEPDAUGHTER (*coming forward as if in a trance*): Yes, what he
says is true. . . . I would go and tempt him. . . . There, in his
gloomy study. . . . Just at twilight. . . . He would be sitting
there, sunk in an armchair. . . . Not bothering to stir himself
and switch on the light. . . . Content to let the room get darker
and darker. . . . Until the whole room was filled with a darkness that was alive with our presence. . . . We were there to
tempt him. . . . (*And then, as if she saw herself as still in that study
and irritated by the presence of all those actors.*) Oh, go away. . . .
All of you! Leave us alone! Mummy . . . and her son. . . . I
and the little girl. . . . The boy by himself. . . . Always by
himself. . . . Then he and I together (*a faint gesture in the
direction of the* FATHER). And then. . . . By myself. . . . By
myself . . . alone in that darkness (*a sudden turn round as if she
wished to seize and fix the vision that she has of herself, the living
vision of herself that she sees shining in the darkness*). Yes, my life!
Ah, what scenes, what wonderful scenes we suggested to
him! And I . . . I tempted him more than any of them. . . .

FATHER: Indeed you did! And it may well be that it's all your
fault that he wouldn't give us the life we asked for. . . . You
were too persistent. . . . Too impudent. . . . You exaggerated
too much. . . .

STEPDAUGHTER: What? When it was he who wanted me to be
what I am? (*She goes up to the* PRODUCER *and says confidentially.*)
I think it's much more likely that he refused because he felt
depressed . . . or because of his contempt for the theatre.
. . . Or at least, for the present-day theatre with all its pander-
ing to the box-office. . . .

PRODUCER: Let's get on! Let's get on, for God's sake! Let's
have some action!

STEPDAUGHTER: It looks to me as if we've got too much action
for you already. . . . Just staging our entry into his house
(*pointing to the* FATHER). You yourself said that you couldn't
stick up notices or be changing the set every five minutes.

PRODUCER: And neither can we! Of course we can't! What

we've got to do is to combine and group all the action into one continuous well-knit scene. . . . Not the sort of thing that you want. . . . With, first of all, your younger brother coming home from school and wandering about the house like some lost soul. . . . Hiding behind doors and brooding on a plan that . . . What did you say it does to him?

STEPDAUGHTER: Dries him up. . . . Shrivels him up completely.

PRODUCER: M'm! Well, as you said. . . . And all the time you can see it more and more clearly in his eyes. . . . Wasn't that what you said?

STEPDAUGHTER: Yes. . . . Just look at him! (*Pointing to where he is standing by his* MOTHER.)

PRODUCER: And then, at the same time, you want the child to be playing in the garden, blissfully unaware of everything. The boy in the house, the little girl in the garden. . . . I ask you!

STEPDAUGHTER: Yes . . . happily playing in the sun! That is the only pleasure that I have. . . . Her happiness. . . . All the joy that she gets from playing in the garden. . . . After the wretchedness and the squalor of that horrible room where we all four slept together. . . . And she had to sleep with me. . . Just think of it. . . . My vile contaminated body next to hers. . . . With her holding me tight in her loving, innocent, little arms! She only had to get a glimpse of me in the garden and she'd run up to me and take me by the hand. She wasn't interested in the big flowers . . . she'd run about looking for the . . . 'weeny' ones. . . . So that she could point them out to me. . . . And she'd be so happy. . . . So excited. . . (*As she says this she is torn by the memory of it all and gives a long despairing cry, dropping her head on to her hands which are lying loosely on the little table in front of her. At the sight of her emotion everyone is deeply moved. The* PRODUCER *goes up to her almost paternally and says comfortingly.*)

PRODUCER: We'll have the garden in. . . Don't you worry. . . We'll have the garden scene in. . . . Just you wait and see. . . You'll be quite satisfied with how I arrange it. . . . We'll play everything in the garden. (*Calling a* STAGE-HAND.) Hey (h *name*)! Let me have something in the shape of a tree or two. . . . A couple of not-too-large cypresses in front of this fountain! (*Two small cypress trees descend from the flies. The* FOREMAN *dashes up and fixes them with struts and nails.*)

PRODUCER (*to the* STEPDAUGHTER): That'll do. . . . For the moment anyway. . . . It'll give us a rough idea. (*Calls to the* STAGE-HAND *again.*) Oh (*his name*), let me have something for a sky, will you?

STAGE-HAND (*up aloft*): Eh?

PRODUCER: Something for a sky! A blackcloth to go behind the fountain! (*And a white backcloth descends from the flies.*)

PRODUCER: Not white! I said I wanted a sky! Oh, well, it doesn't matter. . . . Leave it! Leave it! . . . I'll fix it myself. . . . (*Calls.*) Hey! . . . You there on the lights! . . . Everything off. . . . And let me have the moonlight blues on! . . . Blues in the batten! . . . A couple of blue spots on the backcloth! . . . Yes, that's it! That's just right!

(*There is now a mysterious moonlit effect about the scene, and the* ACTORS *are prompted to move about and to speak as they would if they were indeed walking in a moonlit garden.*)

PRODUCER (*to the* STEPDAUGHTER): There, do you see? Now the Boy, instead of hiding behind doors inside the house, can move about the garden and hide behind these trees. But, you know, it'll be rather difficult to find a little girl to play that scene with you. . . . The one where she shows you the flowers. (*Turning to the* BOY.) Now come down here a bit! Let's see how it works out! (*Then, since the* BOY *doesn't move.*) Come on! Come on! (*He drags him forward and tries to make him hold his head up. But after every attempt down it falls again.*) Good God, here's a fine how d'ye do. . . . There's something queer about this boy. . . . What's the matter with him? . . . My God, he'll have to say *something*. . . . (*He goes up to him, puts a hand on his shoulder and places him behind one of the trees.*) Now. . . . Forward a little! . . . Let me see you! . . . M'm! . . . Now hide yourself. . . . That's it! Now try popping your head out a bit . . . Take a look round. . . . (*He goes to one side to study the effect and the* BOY *does what he has been told to do. The* ACTORS *look on, deeply affected and quite dismayed.*) That's excellent! . . . Yes, excellent! (*Turning again to the* STEPDAUGHTER.) Suppose the little girl were to catch sight of him there as he was looking out, and run over to him. . . . Wouldn't that drag a word or two out of him?

STEPDAUGHTER (*rising*): It's no use your hoping that he'll speak. . . . At least not so long as *he's* here (*pointing to the* SON). If you want him to speak, you'll have to send *him* away first.

SON (*going resolutely towards the steps down into the auditorium*): Willingly! I'm only too happy to oblige! Nothing could possibly suit me better!

PRODUCER (*immediately catching hold of him*): Hey! Oh no you don't! Where are you going? You hang on a minute!

(*The* MOTHER *rises in dismay, filled with anguish at the thought that he really is going away. She instinctively raises her arms to prevent him from going, without, however, moving from where she is standing.*)

SON (*he has reached the footlights*): I tell you . . . There's absolutely nothing for me to do here! Let me go, please! Let me go! (*This to the* PRODUCER.)

PRODUCER: What do you mean . . . There's nothing for you to do?

STEPDAUGHTER (*placidly, ironically*): Don't bother to hold him back! He won't go away!

FATHER: He has to play that terrible scene with his Mother in the garden.

SON (*immediately, fiercely, resolutely*): I'm not playing anything! I've said that all along! (*To the* PRODUCER.) Let me go!

STEPDAUGHTER (*running over, then addressing the* PRODUCER): Do you mind? (*She gets him to lower the hand with which he has been restraining the* SON.) Let him go! (*Then turning to the* SON, *as soon as the* PRODUCER *has dropped his arm.*) Well, go on. . . . Leave us!

(*The* SON *stands where he is, still straining in the direction of the steps, but, as if held back by some mysterious force, he cannot go down them. Then, amidst the utter dismay and anxious bewilderment of the* ACTORS, *he wanders slowly along the length of the footlights in the direction of the other flight of steps. Once there, he again finds himself unable to descend, much as he would wish to. The* STEP

DAUGHTER *has watched his progress intently, her eyes challenging, defiant. Now she bursts out laughing.*)

STEPDAUGHTER: He can't, you see! He can't leave us! He must remain here. . . . He has no choice but to remain with us! He's chained to us. . . . Irrevocably! But if I . . . Who really do run away when what is inevitable happens. . . . And I run away because of my hatred for him. . . . I run away just because I can no longer bear the sight of him. . . . Well, if I can still stay here. . . . If I can still put up with his company and with having to have him here before my eyes. . . . Do you think it's likely that he can run away? Why, he has to stay here with that precious father of his. . . . With his mother. . . . Because now she has no other children but him. . . . (*Turning to her* MOTHER.) Come on, Mummy! Come on. . . . (*Turning to the* PRODUCER *and pointing to the* MOTHER.) There. . . . You see. . . . She'd got up to prevent him from going. . . . (*To her* MOTHER, *as if willing her actions by some magic power*.) Come on! Come on! (*Then to the* PRODUCER.) You can imagine just how reluctant she is to give this proof of her affection in front of your actors. But so great is her desire to be with him that . . . There! . . . You see? . . . She's willing to live out again her scene with him! (*And as a matter of fact the* MOTHER *has gone up to her* SON, *and scarcely has the* STEPDAUGHTER *finished speaking before she makes a gesture to indicate her agreement*.)

SON (*immediately*): No! No! You're not going to drag me into this! If I can't get away, I shall stay here! But I repeat that I'm not going to do any acting at all!

FATHER (*trembling with excitement, to the* PRODUCER): You can force him to act!

SON: Nobody can force me!

FATHER: I can and I will!

STEPDAUGHTER: Wait! Wait! First of all the little girl has to go to the fountain. . . . (*Goes over to the* LITTLE GIRL. *She drops on to her knees in front of her and takes her face in her hands*.) Poor little darling. . . . You're looking so bewildered. . . . With those beautiful big eyes. . . . You must be wondering just

where you are. We're on a stage, dear! What's a stage?
Well . . . It's a place where you play at being serious. They
put on plays here. And now *we're* putting a play on. Really
and truly! Even you. . . . (*Embracing her, clasping her to her
breast and rocking her for a moment or so.*) Oh, you little
darling. . . . My dear little darling, what a terrible play for
you. . . . What a horrible end they've thought out for you!
The garden, the fountain. . . . Yes, it's a make-believe fountain. . . . The pity is, darling, that everything's make-believe
here. . . . But perhaps you like a make-believe fountain better
than a real one. . . . So that you can play in it. . . . M'm?
No. . . . It'll be a game for the others. . . . Not for you unfor-
tunately . . . Because you're real. . . . And you really play by
a real fountain. . . . A lovely big green one, with masses of
bamboo palms casting shadows. . . . Looking at your reflection
in the water. . . . And lots and lots of little baby ducklings
swimming about in it, breaking the shadow into a thousand
little ripples. You try to take hold of one of the ducklings. . .
(*With a shriek which fills everybody with dismay.*) No, Rosetta, no!
Your Mummy's not looking after you. . . . And all because of
that swine there. . . . Her son! I feel as if all the devils in hell
were loose inside me. . . . And he . . . (*Leaves the* LITTLE GIRL
and turns with her usual scorn to the BOY.) What are you doing
. . . drooping there like that? . . . Always the little beggar-
boy! It'll be your fault too if that baby drowns. . . . Because
of the way you go on. . . . As if I didn't pay for everybody
when I got you into his house. (*Seizing his arm to make him take
his hand out of his pocket.*) What have you got there? What are
you trying to hide? Out with it! Take that hand out of your
pocket! (*She snatches his hand out of his pocket and to everybody's
horror reveals that it is clenched round a revolver. She looks at him for
a little while, as if satisfied. Then she says sombrely.*) M'm! Where
did you get that gun from? . . . And how did you manage
to lay your hands on it? (*And since the* BOY, *in his utter dismay—
his eyes are staring and vacant—does not reply.*) You idiot! If I'd
been you I shouldn't have killed myself. . . . I'd have killed one
of *them*. . . . Or the pair of them! Father and son together!

(*She hides him behind the cypress tree where he was lurking before. Then she takes the* LITTLE GIRL *by the hand and leads her towards the fountain. She puts her into the basin of the fountain, and makes her lie down so that she is completely hidden. Finally she goes down on her knees and buries her head in her hands on the rim of the basin of the fountain.*)

PRODUCER: That's it! Good! (*Turning to the* SON.) And at the same time. . . .

SON (*angrily*): What do you mean . . . 'And at the same time'? Oh, no! . . . Nothing of the sort! There never was any scene between her and me! (*Pointing to the* MOTHER.) You make her tell you what really happened! (*Meanwhile the* SECOND ACTRESS *and the* JUVENILE LEAD *have detached themselves from the group of* ACTORS *and are standing gazing intently at the* MOTHER *and the* SON *so that later they can act these parts.*)

MOTHER: Yes, it's true, sir! I'd gone to his room at the time.

SON: There! Did you hear? To my room! Not into the garden!

PRODUCER: That doesn't matter at all! As I said we'll have to run all the action together into one composite scene!

SON (*becoming aware that the* JUVENILE LEAD *is studying him*): What do *you* want?

JUVENILE LEAD: Nothing! I was just looking at you.

SON (*turning to the* SECOND ACTRESS): Oh! . . . And *you're* here too, are you? All ready to play *her* part, I suppose? (*Pointing to the* MOTHER.)

PRODUCER: That's the idea! And if you want my opinion you ought to be damned grateful for all the attention they're paying you.

SON: Indeed? Thank you! But hasn't it dawned on you yet that you aren't going to be able to stage this play? Not even the tiniest vestige of us is to be found in you. . . . And all the time your actors are studying us from the outside. Do you think it's possible for us to live confronted by a mirror which, not merely content with freezing us in that particular picture which is the fixing of our expression, has to throw an image back at us which we can no longer recognise? . . . Our own features, yes. . . . But twisted into a horrible grimace.

FATHER: He's quite right! He's quite right, you know!

PRODUCER (*to the* JUVENILE LEAD *and* SECOND ACTRESS): Right you are! Get back with the others!

SON: It's no use your bothering! I'm not having anything to do with this!

PRODUCER: You be quiet for the moment, and let me listen to what your mother has to say! (*To the* MOTHER.) You were saying? . . . You'd gone to his room? . . .

MOTHER: Yes, I'd gone to his room. . . . . I couldn't bear the strain any longer! I wanted to pour out my heart to him. . . . I wanted to tell him of all the anguish that was tormenting me. . . . But as soon as he saw me come in . . .

SON: There was no scene between us! I rushed out of the room. . . . I didn't want to get involved in any scenes! Because I never have been involved in any! Do you understand?

MOTHER: Yes! That *is* what happened! That is what happened.

PRODUCER: But for the purposes of this play we've simply *got* to have a scene between you and him! Why . . . it's absolutely *essential*!

MOTHER: I'm quite ready to take part in one! Oh, if you could only find some way to give me an opportunity of speaking to him . . . if only for a moment. . . . So that I can pour out my heart to him!

FATHER (*going up to the* SON, *in a great rage*): You'll do what she asks, do you understand? You'll do what your Mother asks!

SON (*more stubbornly than ever*): I'm doing nothing!

FATHER (*taking hold of him by the lapels of his coat and shaking him*): My God, you'll do what I tell you! Or else . . . Can't you hear how she's pleading with you? Haven't you a spark of feeling in you for your Mother?

SON (*grappling with the* FATHER): No, I haven't! For God's sake let's have done with all this. . . . Once and for all, let's have done with it!

(*General agitation. The* MOTHER *is terrified and tries to get between them in order to separate them.*)

MOTHER: Please! *Please!*

FATHER (*without relinquishing his hold*): You must obey me! You *must!*

SON (*struggling with him and finally hurling him to the ground. He falls near the steps amidst general horror*): What's come over you? Why are you in this terrible state of frenzy? Haven't you any sense of decency? . . . Going about parading your shame. . . . And ours, too. I'm having nothing to do with this affair! Nothing, do you hear? And by making this stand I am interpreting the wishes of our author, who didn't wish to put us on the stage!

PRODUCER: Oh, God! You come along here and . . .

SON (*pointing to the* FATHER): He did! I didn't!

PRODUCER: Aren't you here now?

SON: It was he who wanted to come. . . . And he dragged us all along with him. Then the pair of them went in there with you and agreed on what was to go into the play. But he didn't only stick to what really did occur. . . . No, as if that wasn't enough for any man, he had to put in things that never even happened.

PRODUCER: Well, then, you tell me what really happened! You can at least do that! You rushed out of your room without saying a word?

SON (*he hesitates for a moment*): Without saying a word! I didn't want to get involved in a scene!

PRODUCER (*pressing him*): And then? What did you do then?

SON (*everybody's attention is on him; amidst the anguished silence he takes a step or two across the front of the stage*): Nothing. . . . As I was crossing the garden . . . (*he breaks off and becomes gloomy and absorbed*).

PRODUCER (*urging him to speak, very much moved by this extraordinary reserve*): Well? As you were crossing the garden?

SON (*in exasperation, shielding his face with his arm*): Why do you want to force me to tell you? It's horrible!

(*The* MOTHER *is trembling all over and stifled sobs come from her as she looks towards the fountain.*)

PRODUCER (*slowly, quietly . . . he has seen where the* MOTHER *is looking and he now turns to the* SON *with growing apprehension*): The little girl?

SON (*staring straight in front of him, out into the auditorium*): There . . . In the fountain. . . .

FATHER (*from where he is on the floor, pointing with tender pity to the* MOTHER): She was following him. . . .

PRODUCER (*anxiously to the* SON): And what did you do?

SON (*slowly, continuing to stare in front of him*): I rushed up to the fountain. . . . I was about to dive in and fish her out. . . . Then all of a sudden I pulled up short. . . . Behind that tree I saw something that made my blood run cold. . . . The boy. . . . The boy was standing there. . . . Stock still. . . . With madness in his eyes. . . . Staring like some insane creature at his little sister, who was lying drowned in the fountain! (*The* STEP-DAUGHTER, *who has all this while been bent over the fountain in order to hide the* LITTLE GIRL, *is sobbing desperately—her sobs coming like an echo from the background. There is a pause.*) I moved towards him. . . . And then . . . (*And from behind the trees where the* BOY *is hidden a revolver shot rings out.*)

MOTHER (*with a heartrending cry she rushes behind the trees accompanied by the* SON *and all the* ACTORS. *There is general confusion*): Oh, my son! My son! (*And then amidst the general hubbub and shouting.*) Help! Oh, help!

PRODUCER (*amidst all the shouting, he tries to clear a space while the* BOY *is carried off behind the skycloth*): Is he wounded? Is he badly hurt?

(*By now everybody, except for the* PRODUCER *and the* FATHER, *who is still on the ground by the steps, has disappeared behind the skycloth. They can be heard muttering and exclaiming in great consternation. Then first from one side, then from the other, the* ACTORS *re-enter.*)

LEADING LADY (*re-entering right, very much moved*): He's dead, poor boy! He's dead! Oh what a terrible thing to happen!

LEADING MAN (*re-entering left, laughing*): What do you mean, dead? It's all make-believe! It's all just a pretence! Don't get taken in by it!

OTHER ACTORS (*entering from the right*): Make-believe? Pretence? Reality! Reality! He's dead!

OTHERS (*from the left*): No! Make-believe! It's all a pretence!

FATHER (*rising and crying out to them*): What do you mean, pretence? Reality, ladies and gentlemen, reality! Reality! (*And desperation in his face, he too disappears behind the backcloth*).

PRODUCER (*at the end of his tether*): Pretence! Reality! Go to hell, the whole lot of you! Lights! Lights! Lights!

(*The stage and the auditorium are suddenly flooded with very bright light. The* PRODUCER *breathes again as if freed from a tremendous burden. They all stand there looking into one another's eyes, in an agony of suspense and dismay.*)

PRODUCER: My God! Nothing like this has ever happened to me before! I've lost a whole day on their account! (*He looks at his watch.*) You can go home now. . . . All of you! There's nothing we can do now! It's too late to start rehearsing again! I'll see you all this evening. (*And as soon as the* ACTORS *have said 'Goodbye!' and gone he calls out to the* ELECTRICIAN.) Hey (*his name*)! Everything off! (*He has hardly got the words out before the theatre is plunged for a moment into utter darkness.*) Hell! You might at least leave me one light on, so that I can see where I'm going!

And immediately behind the backcloth, a green flood lights up. It projects the silhouettes of the CHARACTERS (*minus the* BOY *and the* LITTLE GIRL), *clear-cut and huge, on to the backcloth. The* PRODUCER *is terrified and leaps off the stage. As he does so the green flood is switched off—rather as if its having come on in the first instance had been due to the* ELECTRICIAN'S *having pulled the wrong switch—and the stage is again lit in blue. Slowly the* CHARACTERS *come in and advance to the front of the stage. The* SON *comes in first, from the right, followed by the* MOTHER, *who has her arms outstretched towards him. Then the* FATHER *comes in from the left. They stop half-way down the stage and stand there like people in a trance. Last of all the* STEPDAUGHTER *comes in from the left and runs towards the steps which lead down into the auditorium. With her foot on the top step she stops for a moment to look at the other three and bursts into strident laughter. Then she hurls herself down the steps and runs up the aisle. She stops at the back of the auditorium and turns to look at the three figures standing on the stage. She bursts*

out laughing again. And when she has disappeared from the audi-
torium you can still hear her terrible laughter coming from the foyer
beyond. A short pause and then,

CURTAIN